Mentoring

'*Mentoring* brings the heart of relational leadership into practice with great sensitivity and deep insight borne from both personal experience and study.'

Pat Patterson, Program Director, Warm Beach Christian Conference Center, Washington

'If you have never had a wise mentor, hitch up to the rope through this book! In its pages you will find all you need to know to get started in a new adventure of lifelong, reciprocal learning.'

Dr Shirley H. Showalter, President of Goshen College, Goshen

'An excellent volume for those considering a mentoring relationship, and those who wish to be more deeply and more meaningfully involved in such a relationship.'

Peter Chao, President of Eagles Communications, Singapore

'This is a book of story telling – of lives blessed by mentoring relationships across cultures, gender, and professions. You will be inspired, motivated, and challenged by this gifted mentor as all his privileged mentorees have been.'

Patricia Chiu, China Graduate School of Theology, Hong Kong

'Dr Wright's book is full of priceless experience and keen insight – a product of a lifetime of thinking through and practicing the art of giving and receiving as mentor and mentoree. Its authentic voice will encourage and help all who are interested in the journey of finding or becoming a mentor.'

Dr Uli H. Chi, Chairman, Computer Human Interaction, LLC, Seattle, Washington

'This book challenges, questions and encourages all of us in leadership to honour and value people who come into our lives... The definitive book on mentoring so far.'

Dr Neale Fong, Chief Executive Officer, St John of God Health Care, West Perth

Mentoring

The Promise of Relational Leadership

Walter C. Wright, Jr.

Foreword by
Max De Pree

PATERNOSTER

10 09 08 07 06 05 04   8 7 6 5 4 3 2 1

First published 2004 by Paternoster Press
Paternoster Press is a division of Authentic Media
9 Holdom Avenue, Bletchley, Milton Keynes, Bucks,
MK1 1QR, UK
and PO Box 1047, Waynesboro, GA 30830-2047
www.authenticmedia.co.uk

British Library Cataloguing in Publication Data

A catalogue record for this book is available from the
British Library

ISBN 1-84227-293-4

Cover design by 4-9-0 ltd
Print Management by Adare Carwin
Printed and bound by AIT Nørhaven A/S, Denmark

Contents

110601

Foreword

One of society's significant needs is the continuous development and maturation of its leaders. Based on many years of mentoring and being mentored, I believe this give-and-take relationship is the most effective way to guide people with leadership gifts toward their potential. Mentor was the trusted friend whom Odysseus left in charge of Ithaca as he departed for the Trojan War. Disguised as Mentor, the goddess Athena helps Telemachus, Odysseus's son, search for his father. Through the centuries, the word has come to mean trusted advisor and counselor, and the mentoring relationship today seems to me to have become a primary way to grow and develop as a leader.

A wonderful variety of people are candidates for mentoring. There are people dealing with the unexpected demands of promotion and people who decide to shift from the for-profit world to the non-profit world. There are young people – teachers, pastors, or managers – early in their careers and people finishing up one career and exploring another. There are folks surprised by failure. There are people in academia, especially, who move from a specialized discipline to administrative or leadership responsibilities. There are volunteers searching for new meaning in life. Mentoring can succeed at various stages in life.

The needs of mentors and mentorees are both challenging. Our purpose in writing these thoughts and ideas and experiences is to encourage legions more of seasoned leaders to lend their wisdom to this calling. For those approaching retirement, mentoring is a life-giving way of being called to retirement, rather than defaulting to retirement. For those still engaged in the daunting job of active leadership, mentoring is a way to bring all the advantages of contemplation and unbiased perspective to an active life.

Mentoring takes place in many settings and at many levels. I would like to increase the value of my experiences in mentoring by drawing some guidelines, some rules, and some practices from them that I hope you will find helpful and encouraging as you ponder the role of mentor or mentoree. Mentoring cannot be reduced to a formula. All we can do is build a framework on which we can hang our experiences, gifts, and art in such a way that another person can interact with it, make sense of it, take ownership of it, and work at reaching new levels of humanity and leadership on their own.

Mentoring is above all a work of love, which at its best is a two-way exchange. Though both parties walk away with priceless insights, both people come to each other intent on giving rather than taking. The immediate goal of mentoring is reaching toward potential. It thrives in community and prospers with risk – for nothing worthwhile arrives without risk. It thrives on the vulnerability of both mentor and mentoree. It focuses on the whys and wherefores in our work and our lives, not on the what and the how. Mentoring is about conjugating the verb "to be," not the verb "to have," to paraphrase the pianist

Franz Liszt, himself a famous mentor. Mentoring is not a private management seminar. Its ultimate goal is to make mentors out of mentorees.

Mentoring is a holistic approach to becoming a better servant – to one's calling, to one's society, to one's followers. It has to do with family and career. Its roots lie in ethical behavior and virtuous beliefs. Mentors and mentorees work hard at establishing and nurturing relationships. They respect the value of effective communication.

At its best, mentoring is a covenantal approach to life and leadership. I once heard a wonderful description of the work of a mentor: A bird doesn't sing because it has an answer. It sings because it has a song.

Over a long working life, I had many teachers to whom I am indebted. Carl Frost, David Hubbard and Peter Drucker are the three chief mentors in my life. Carl Frost was a professor at Michigan State University and consultant to Herman Miller, Inc. for more than forty-five years. During much of that time, he was also my mentor. His field was Industrial Psychology, and he was one of the earliest and foremost proponents of participative management.

For thirty years David Hubbard was the President of Fuller Theological Seminary in Pasadena, California. I served as a member of Fuller Board of Trustees for most of David's tenure. One of his great contributions to my life and to the life of my family was to help me learn how to integrate work into faith.

Peter Drucker was consultant to the management team at Herman Miller for many years. During that time, we became friends and he became my mentor.

Each of these three teachers strongly emphasized in words and actions the critical matter of learning how to establish and nurture good relationships as one of the primary skills of an effective leader. Their mentoring – I would almost rather say their ministering – in my life has been absolutely crucial to my development as a leader and to the quality of my family's life.

Beginning in the early 1980s, I myself became a mentor. Like many important parts of life, my mentoring became central without my realizing it. Over the years, around twenty people have been gracious enough to ask me to meet with them about mentoring. I'm not exactly sure how all the relationships started, but I can tell you that at this stage in my life I'm sure glad they did start. I have been involved with folks from non-profit organizations – most often in education and government – and from for-profit organizations, including people from manufacturing, investment banking, and publishing. With only one exception, my mentoring relationships have all been long-term working relationships. Most of these people have gone on to become mentors to others. As you can imagine, I have learned a good deal from these friends – for my mentorees have all become my friends – and our experiences together.

Mentoring relationships can begin in a variety of ways. Getting to know each other is, of course, a given. In my experience, a mentoring relationship does not begin from scratch. It blooms after the flower has been cultivated for a while. You suddenly find yourself discussing with someone you have known the possibility that your meetings might become more intentional, more directed. Usually the mentoree suggests formalizing some arrangement, or at least begins to ask for more time together. Occasionally a mentoring relationship starts without any discussion at all. Sometimes it is at the suggestion of a mutual friend that "you ought to consider talking with so-and-so about that." But there always comes a time when both people feel that a talk about mutual commitments is a good idea. Sometimes it is practical to approach someone and ask her or him to be your mentor, but to make mentoring work between strangers is quite demanding.

Mentoring is about life-long learning. The kind of world most of us live in makes life-long learning a natural requirement, regardless of our discipline or profession or occupation. It's not only a requirement, it's fun. Curiosity isn't limited to mentorees, you know. Expansion of the mind changes attitudes, makes possible new horizons, surprises us concerning our own potential, and often helps us gain essential skills of finding and developing relationships. This last result of learning is crucial because so few of us work independently, and poor relationships can seriously diminish personal and professional competence in a leader's life.

Many of us struggle with life-long learning. We have access to more information than we can possibly use. We struggle to translate information into knowledge, and we seek to explain to ourselves how to transform knowledge into wisdom. This progression becomes another emphasis for a mentor: a field of exploration best approached with questions and not with answers. One of the best ways of giving guidance in the self-development of mentorees has to be the especially apposite question, the arresting query. It is the Socratic approach.

An important aspect of the mentor's responsibility is to be diligent in guiding discussion away from "What shall I do?" and toward "Who do I intend to be?" What we do in life will always be a consequence of who we are. The mentor and the mentoree have joined together in a process of becoming.

Mentors guide personal development by formulating questions that trigger responsive thought, that bring the light of experience to the discussion and that encourage breadth rather than narrow focus. Mentors have the opportunity to move the interaction beyond job or career into family matters, other areas of service, or areas of study not connected to career. We all ought to know something special – about the arts, about theology or philosophy, about other cultures. One very specific reason to broaden the horizons of our discussions is to remove the fear I have found in many leaders of the creative process and creative people. For organizations that depend on creating change through innovation, such fear is a serious threat. As mentor and mentoree move more deeply and intimately into a relationship of real trust and confidence, our personal uniqueness leads to an expansion of the ground we cover and a comfort with exploring new and unfamiliar territory.

It seems to me that these thoughts about mentoring lead us naturally to think about the personal chemistry needed to make mentoring enticing and productive. My experience tells me that we need a good deal of common ground on which to build a mentoring relationship: shared philosophy, familiar experience, and an easiness with each other's language. We need confidence and respect in common. The mentor should believe in the potential and commitment of the mentoree. We should be in the process for the long haul.

Our working modus begins with candor. We understand clearly that mutual trust and confidentiality are the order of the day. The process must be objective and disciplined; pandering and flattery must be absent. We must agree to hold each other accountable.

Are there ground rules we might consider? Here are a few. You will surely discover more.

For instance, we should be prepared to live with a certain level of ambiguity, even mystery. Leadership in some ways is like being a parent of a 17-year old. You don't have to know everything. We don't need to share everything for us to help each other. Much about human potential remains a mystery. As mentors, we don't need grades or progress reports to be effective. Our mentorees are already mature, effective adults who have accepted responsibility for their own development.

Don't expect miracles. Mentoring is not problem solving; it is growing together. Be a bit laid back. Don't expect concrete changes from visit to visit. Remember, mentorees also hold down jobs and may already have a boss or a board with high expectations.

Another good rule of thumb is that to be a good mentor we need more than desire and theory. The mentor's side of the bargain is to be competent and a good communicator. Competence comes from ex- perience: don't go to sea with a captain who has never left port. Competence is never unlimited: don't try to give help in areas of your incompetence. (It's tempting sometimes to think that one's position as mentor conveys omniscience!) Every mentoree deserves a mentor's best shot, part of which surely includes good communication, by which I mean the ability to listen and a knack for telling stories from experience.

Be prepared to surrender some privacy. You will, on occasion, receive a phone call during dinner. You should trust your mentoree to decide when a subject can't wait until business hours. If he/she calls after dinner, be prepared to go to work. It must be important.

Finally, what about compensation? As I said earlier, I think of mentoring as a work of love. Taking money for it seems to me to be a contradiction. Consulting requires compensation, for the intended results of consulting are so very different from those of mentoring. There may be situations that would lead you to make a different judgment. I only suggest you consider carefully the effects of linking compensation and mentoring.

Let me share some thoughts about the actual practice of mentoring. Here are some of the nuts and bolts of making this process work.

It's important to know each other face to face. You can accomplish a good deal on the phone or through email, but a working intimacy with each other is essential. When you are apart, both people need to visualize the other person's geography and circumstances.

Cover the basics early. Who travels? Who initiates contact? My answer is the mentoree. Who sets the agenda? The mentoree. The mentor is obligated to keep good notes so that he/she can be properly prepared for future discussions. Mentoring, after all, is not an off-the-cuff proposition. How shall we express the goals for this relationship? I suggest you freely discuss them together; the terms of your mutual agreement should be agreed upon together.

The process of mentoring may be enjoyable, but good mentoring is not easy work for either person. While mentors should not ordinarily follow up or seek out performance measurement, it is certainly reasonable to expect real perseverance on the part of the mentoree. Personal growth is a serious business. It requires determination, grit, and heart.

While a mentor does not usually follow up on suggestions or performance, some exceptions need mentioning. A certain discipline is in order. Repeated discussions of the same problem are not constructive. Laying blame elsewhere as an excuse needs to be avoided. Getting together without an agenda can be a pleasant social experience, but it is not mentoring. It's important to have both kinds of time together, but don't confuse them. When sessions are face to face, it's helpful to share a meal and have snacks and drinks available. Eating together is an important part of mentoring transactions.

Sometimes we need to work around detours. Family matters – rightly so – can interrupt. A job offer to your mentoree may seem like a distraction at first. Organizational politics intrude, or a subordinate of your mentoree seriously disappoints. A critical performance review by a board of directors can become a setback. It's important to see these events as perfectly normal parts of a mentoring relationship. Work with them as opportunities to learn and develop; don't overreact to them as emergencies.

Occasionally a mentoree simply moves on. There is no disagreement or conflict; your mentoree simply stops calling. This, too, is OK. Mentorees have a right to move on. In some cases, they no longer need your help. Some retire. Sometimes their resolve weakens. Some become mentors – which we always hope for – and their attention shifts. Whatever the case, your own experience and energy and time are now available to someone else.

Of course, sometimes mentors fail. As we get older, it's more and more difficult to be perfect, don't you think? Sometimes mentoring relationships fail because one person becomes too passive, and a challenge is ignored rather than exploited. Sometimes disagreements crop up that indicate the two of us ought to try other paths of growth. As we work together, sometimes we discover that we disagree as to goals or philosophy or potential. Or we find that our chemistry together isn't what we thought it might become, and we agree to part. These kinds of failures are not the end of life; they are part of life. Mentoring, like so many worthwhile things, is risky. We should realize the risk every time we begin a mentoring relationship and discover how necessary risk and failure are to learning.

Try to remember that mentoring is a process of becoming, not an unimpeded march to perfection. The odds of success increase tremendously when we understand that mutual discovery, not exclusive answers, leads to potential. The best mentors spark the discovery.

Several of the persons who call me mentor have decided to work together to further the practice of mentoring. At one of their sessions in June of 2002, they set aside a part of their meeting to thank me for my own efforts at helping them discover the best about themselves. In many ways, it was an embarrassing morning as one after another spoke in wonderful ways about our times together. Each of them brought me a unique gift that symbolized for them the very special relationship that mentoring can become. Walter Wright gave me a karabiner – a piece of mountain climbing equipment used to connect people by rope. This particular karabiner had been on a trek to the Mount Everest Base Camp and Kala Pataar at over 18,000 feet and back down. The gift and accompanying words – like the other gifts and words that day – made my eyes water. It reminded me of the power and love and growth that spring from simple human connections.

Max De Pree
Holland, Michigan

Introduction

Wisdom for the journey

Ropes and relationships

Mountaineering has been an important part of my life and leadership development. I have been part of a group of men who have climbed mountains together for 29 years. I find in mountaineering a rich resource for analogies of leadership and management, relationships and community. Almost every element of leadership and organizational life finds an image or metaphor present in the organization and execution of a mountaineering expedition.

The mountaineering rope has been an especially powerful image for me – the connection between climbers at high altitude. The process of roping up is a metaphor that helps me think about leadership – an image that informs my thinking about mentoring.

The rope is a powerful image of connection, but it makes a rather bulky gift. So when I needed a symbolic gift to give to my mentor, Max De Pree, I chose a very personal symbol: the karabiner – the personal hardware with which each individual climber ties into the climbing rope. The karabiner I gave him had served me since my introductory mountaineering course with the Sierra Club. With it I tied into rope teams that climbed Mt. Rainier and Mt. Baker in the Washington Cascades, Mt. Banner, North Peak, and several attempts on Mt. Ritter in the California Sierras. As Max notes, I took this karabiner to the Mount Everest Base Camp.

The karabiner is the clip that ties a mountaineer into a climbing rope. Being roped up is about tying your life to another – an image that fuels my understanding of mentoring. As we begin to think about mentoring, here are some seed thoughts from the metaphor of being roped up.

- *The rope is the mountaineer's lifeline.* It distributes the risk among a group; it provides a layer of protection for the individual. It reminds climbers that they are not alone. Others share this journey; others have the same goal. The rope keeps us connected.
- *Climbers choose to rope up.* It is for their own protection – against mistakes and bad decisions. In the 1970s, the BBC sponsored a climb up Mt. Everest. The first team of Doug Scott and Dougal Hasten successfully reached the top. The second team, Martin Boysten and Mick Burke, were nearly there when Boysten's oxygen failed. He had to return to camp. Mick Burke, so close to his personal objective, untied from the climbing rope and proceeded toward the summit alone. He died in that attempt.[1] The climbing rope protects individual climbers from hidden crevasses and from their own bad judgment. Climbers also choose to rope up for the safety of others. One climber in a good position can hold several colleagues secure on a high glacier. However, there is risk involved in tying yourself to another. Another's fall can also take you

down. Recently on Mt. Hood in Oregon, the leader slipped and took two rope teams down. Three died.

- *The strongest climber goes first.* The strongest climber leads the climb, choosing the route and demonstrating the way forward. The lead climber provides security for those following, but leading on a rope is the riskiest position. The lead climber has the furthest to fall before the followers can stop him or her. Recently a group of paraplegics climbed Mt. Shasta in California. One member of the team was Mark Wellman. Wellman received fame several years ago when he climbed the 3,000 foot rock wall of El Capitan in Yosemite Valley. It was a major achievement for one who was "never to climb again." But it was Mike Corbett who had caught my attention in the original story. Mike Corbett risked his life by roping himself to a paraplegic and coaching his friend up that awesome rock face.

- *Being roped to someone stronger protects you against your mistakes.* The lead climber holds you secure while you correct (learn) and recover. It also encourages risk. It is much easier to risk when you know someone will keep you from a fatal fall. Being "roped up" gives confidence, but also means giving *trust*. Actually, you need to fall at least once to learn how to trust.[2]

- *The leader does not do your climbing.* Everyone climbs for himself or herself, even when in trouble. The rope gives you space and time to do what you need to do to get back on your feet.

- *Persons roped together have to find a pace that works.* If the leader walks too fast, the follower is pulled off balance. If the follower walks too slowly, the leader is pulled off balance. If the leader walks too slowly or the follower too fast, the rope gets too much slack and becomes dangerous to both.

- Few climbers have the confidence (or foolishness) to climb on high mountain glaciers without being roped to at least one other person.

For over twenty years I have had the wonderful experience of metaphorically being tied into a rope with my mentor Max De Pree: following a leader who knows who he is, who shows me a path and models a way of climbing: a leader who believes in me enough to let me clip into his rope and to risk a piece of his legacy in my leadership journey. Max De Pree has been a mentor who encourages me to risk learning and growing and leading. He "held" me and believed in me when I fell and thought I was failing. He provides a space to test my ideas, to explore my thinking and review my mistakes. He asks me the questions that I do not think to ask or have been avoiding.

For over twenty years, knowing that Max was only a rope length away gave me the confidence to risk this adventure we call leadership. If the rope is a metaphor of the relationship between mentor and mentoree, the karabiner, for me, is a symbol of the personal choice and connection we have to that mentoring relationship – the choice to learn from a mentor, and the choice to be a mentor.

Sherpas and guides

Max De Pree says that mentoring focuses on who we want to be, not what we want to do. Mentors guide us along this path of thinking. This is a truth I learned also in the mountains. As a climber of mountains, one of the things I have always wanted to do was trek to the Mount Everest Base Camp. In 1998 I had the opportunity to achieve this goal. But even here, hiking over 18,000 feet in the Himalayan mountains of Nepal, my mentors underscored the wisdom of Max De Pree's focus: trekking, like life and leadership, is about who we intend to be more than about what we accomplish.

In the mountains above Kathmandu the best mentors are Sherpas: the men and women who know the mountains, have walked the trails before, who point the way and carry the loads for trekkers and climbers on their journeys. These gentle people, living high in the Himalayas, are known for their remarkable endurance, their expertise as guides, and the amount of oxygen their blood carries. While we normal mortals are gasping for oxygen in the thin air, the Sherpas are carrying their weight or more in baskets hanging from their heads. Sherpas are also very wise about matters of mountain climbing and daily living.

On our trek we had three Sherpa guides: Jamyang, Santosh, and Suresh. I grew to appreciate them greatly over our time together. They gave us important advice and modeled it as we walked the mountains together. There are three lessons I learned from the Sherpas that I believe are foundational to thinking about mentors and mentoring. Three lessons the Sherpas underlined at the beginning and modeled throughout the trip:

1. Walk your own pace.
2. It's the journey that matters, not how high or how far you can go.
3. The people you serve are more important than the summits you climb.

Three truths about trekking; three lessons for life; three foundational assumptions of the mentoring process.

Walk your own pace

Long before the trek even began, this was the mantra repeated over and over by the guides: "Walk your own pace. You do not have to keep up with anyone. You don't have to be Edmund Hillary or Junko Tabei.[3] Be yourself. Walk the pace that is comfortable for you. If you push yourself faster than your pace, you will waste your strength. But, similarly, if you walk slower than your pace, you will also burn off your energy. You have nothing to prove by how fast you go. Be yourself – and walk your own pace!" Wise advice, with application far beyond a mere trek in the mountains.

We heard this advice from the Sherpas every day as they encouraged us up the mountain trail. And they reinforced it with their leadership. As we climbed into the Himalayas one of the guides would go in front leading the way, keeping a pace always a little faster than the fastest trekker. In this way he was always in place to point the direction, to make sure the trail was safe, to keep anyone from wandering off on a wrong path, and to prepare for our next stop. At the same time, a second Sherpa always came behind, following the group, watching for stragglers, encouraging the slower walkers, and making sure that everyone, even the slowest, felt like part of the group. An appropriate pace was anywhere between the lead Sherpa and the following Sherpa, and you could not walk faster than the lead guide nor slower than the following one. The third Sherpa walked with us, talking and encouraging everyone as we moved at our own pace, pointing out sights and animals, naming the mountains and villages, monitoring the condition of the trekkers, and working to see that we got the most out of our daily experience. No matter where we were on the trail, we were always part of the group; we were always included and encouraged. We always belonged. We were surrounded by leadership. This is mentoring at its best.

It is hard for me to reflect on this three-part model of leadership and mentoring – going before, going with and following behind – without thinking of the most famous Biblical psalm. The well-known Twenty-third Psalm falls into three parts: the Shepherd Lord leading God's people along the path that God chooses to lush meadows and restful lakes and rivers; then walking with God's people through the ups and downs of life with comfort, encouragement, and kingly protection; and finally personified as goodness and love, following the people of God until they are safely home in his presence.

That is what the Sherpas modeled in their mentoring leadership. They went before us, walked with us and followed up behind to ensure that each one of us could walk at our own pace – just like the psalmist's God does. Everyone walks his or her own pace.

This is a fundamental assumption of the mentoring process. No one walks our journey for us and no one else's pace is appropriate for us. It is our journey. We walk through life and leadership as unique persons created by God. Mentors help us find our own pace. Walk your own pace. Your pace is neither too fast nor too slow. You have nothing to prove; be yourself. It's the only person you can be. And trust your guides. You do not take this journey alone.

The psalmist recognizes that God has already gone on ahead to prepare the trail and will be with him in the good times and the bad times, and he will not let him fall behind. In fact, there is no behind. There is only the next step and the psalmist believes that God takes it with him. To some extent that is also true about the human mentors in our lives. There are people who have walked the path before who can guide us on portions of our journey. They cannot walk for us, but they can walk with us, pointing the way, encouraging us and helping us to understand and learn when we fall behind.

It's the journey that matters, not how high or how far you can go

The Sherpas repeated this second piece of advice almost as much as the first one. From the first day, the Sherpas told us not to focus on the summit as the measure of success. We knew that normally one-third of the trekkers in most groups cannot acclimatize to the elevation in the limited time that we had available. One-third of us would not reach the summit. And consistently the Sherpas refused to talk about distance. Never would any guide refer to miles or kilometers. It was always days. This is partly due to the impact that altitude and elevation gain have on one's ability to measure distance. It takes ten days to walk from Lukla to Lobuche; but it takes four days to walk from Lobuche to Lukla. However, they also did not focus on distance because they were not measuring by destination. They focused on one day at a time. They encouraged us to come for the trek, not the summit. The summit of Kala Pattar above the Everest Base Camp is only one point on the trek – and not everyone going their own pace should expect to go there. If the destination becomes the measure of success, many factors – health, weather, altitude – could make the trek a failure. If the trek *is* the destination, the trip will be a success regardless of how far we go.

I knew this advice. I knew it as someone who has been turned back from several mountain summits because of weather or health or skill. And basically, I have lived most of my life with this philosophy. I really do believe that life is about living – not accomplishments! But on this trip I resisted the truth. I had flown half way around the world to participate in this trek; but I came for the wrong reason. I wanted to go to the Khumbu basin, to climb higher than 18,000 feet and look down on the Everest Base Camp. And I figured that I might not have such an opportunity again. So I focused strongly on the destination and channeled my energy each day to eating, drinking, sleeping, and staying healthy enough for the next day's trek. Without even realizing it, I walked past incredibly beautiful sights focused on staying healthy enough for tomorrow. At 14,000 feet we were snowed in for three days, and faced the high probability that we might not be able to go higher because of deep snow and no visibility. If you read my journal for those nights, you can see me trying to justify why the trip was a success even if we turned around there. It's not very convincing. When I look at my pictures now, I am surprised how beautiful it was where we were snowed in at Dingboche. Yet in my journal I am complaining about the snow, the altitude and the pungent smell of burning yak dung!

I would like to tell you that I had a spiritual epiphany at 14,000 feet, that I recognized the error of my ways, saw the beauty of the past two weeks and went on not needing to reach the summit. Unfortunately, that is not what happened. I had a very difficult time focusing on God or any of the larger issues of life on this trek, and I did not let go of the summit until I had reached it. Only on the way down did I begin to realize that this was an incredibly beautiful country we were passing through, with remarkable villages and wonderful people. Only on the way down did I stop worrying about my health and strength and find time to reflect on what was happening. And then I got depressed. Then I realized that this goal that I have had for years – this trek to the Everest Base Camp was behind me – it was over. The adventure of my life was done. That is a depressing thought!

It took several days back home talking with friends and mentors before I regained perspective and realized what I had done. I had focused on a destination at the expense of the journey. And like all destinations, when I got there I found it was only one more point on the journey – not the end. My need to reach the summit, teamed with my uncertainty about my ability to make it, focused all of my energy on tomorrow to the extent that I did not enjoy today. So I think I'll just have to go back and do it again – the right way! Which also means that I realize the journey continues, and God knows what adventures still lie ahead!

This too is a foundational assumption of the mentoring process. We are on a journey – a journey of life and leadership. Mentors, like Sherpas, keep reminding us that it is the journey that matters, not how high or how far we can go. There will be peaks and valleys, high points and low times along the journey. The measure of our life and our leadership will be the quality with which we walk the journey, the character with which we engage the people around us, not what we accomplish along the way. It does not matter what we accomplish or where we go. What matters is how we walk and with whom we walk. Our trek is about living. Summits are a distraction. I agree with the psalmist: I believe our destination ultimately is God – the one who goes before us, walks with us, and follows behind, keeping God's people together.

The people you serve are more important than the summits you climb

As we move into a discussion about mentoring it will be clear that much teaching and learning goes on without our knowledge. People watch people of character, particularly people in leadership positions. They observe and draw conclusions from action and behavior as much as from words and direction. We teach with our lives, unconscious of the reality that people are watching and learning. The third lesson I learned from the Sherpas comes from observing their action rather than hearing their advice. And yet it is the obvious corollary to focusing on the journey.

Suresh was the youngest Sherpa. He was a first-year business student at the university in Kathmandu. He had been on many treks before as porter and apprentice, but this was his first trek as a guide. He was the assistant Sirdar, the assistant guide, and manager of the porters. He watched over us with great care, as Jamyang and Santosh watched over him. He took his turn leading, walking with us and following behind, always smiling, always encouraging. It was clear to all of us that the Sherpas were there to serve us. They were more interested in guiding us safely along the trail than achieving the summit. They wanted us to enjoy each day in their country whether or not we reached the Base Camp. Each Sherpa formed a unique relationship with every trekker. Suresh's warm smile, ready wit and natural knowledge made him a welcome companion along the trail. I would have liked to share the excitement of reaching the summit with Suresh. But Suresh did not make it to the summit of Kala Pattar. He did not get to the Khumbu Valley on this trek. When one of the trekkers, Kristina, became ill at 16,000 feet, Suresh stayed behind and escorted her down to the nearest hospital, seeing that she was cared for until we descended. The summit was not important. Kristina was. And to this day, Kristina thinks that Suresh was the best guide on our trek. He was there to assist us on our journey, whether it meant helping someone up a steep portion of trail or helping

Kristina down to the hospital. Suresh, like all of our guides, understood that serving the people with whom he walked was more important than the summits he climbed.

Again, this is a foundational assumption of mentoring, especially for leaders. Leadership is a relationship – a relationship of influence. It is an investment of ourselves in others to influence their vision, values, behaviors, or actions. Leaders exist to serve the people who look to them for leadership, to help the followers realize their potential so that they may successfully contribute to the mission that brings leader and follower together. Leadership is not about the leader. Mentoring is not about the mentor. It is about the people served.

Mentors, like Sherpas, are not there to climb mountains. They are there to assist others on their own journeys, to help them find their pace, to realize their potential, to reflect on what is important in their life and leadership. The paths we walk are filled with other trekkers, pilgrims, men and women traveling through life seeking to understand the events of each day. Many of these are potential mentors or Sherpas – men and women who can walk with us for portions of the trip, sharing from their wisdom and experience, ready to help us up rocky places and down slippery slopes.

Likewise, each one of us is a potential mentor, a Sherpa who understands a portion of the path. None of us has yet finished the journey; we have not arrived. But we have traveled this far. We have wisdom and experience to share as we walk with others. Again, our journey is about service. I believe the final measure of our life will be the people we serve – not the summits we climb. This is the promise of the mentoring relationship.

Mentoring

This is a book about mentoring. It is also the story of one person's journey. Over the past sixty years a wonderful variety of men and women have entered my life as mentors and mentorees – guiding, challenging, encouraging, affirming, and questioning. From these wise Sherpas I have learned much about leadership, relationships, faith, and life. In the pages that follow, I invite you to join me on a journey reflecting on what I have learned about mentors and mentoring from the mentors and mentorees who have graced my life.

Chapter 1 begins with three questions to frame our thinking about the mentoring process. Mentoring is a strategy for leadership development, for personal leadership renewal. It fits within the larger context of relational leadership. Leadership is a relationship of influence that connects the character of the leader with the culture of the community and ultimately impacts the bottom line productivity of the organization. Mentors encourage leaders to reflect on who they are (pace), what is important (journey) and how they are shaping the culture of their organization (relationships).

In the second chapter we will return to Max De Pree, the writer of the book's Foreword. Max De Pree has been a significant mentor in my life – not my first mentor and probably not my last, but the mentor with whom I began to reflect on the mentoring process as an important strategy for leadership development, leadership renewal, and leadership succession. Much of the mentoring model developed in this book was articulated in a twenty-year learning conversation with Max De Pree. It is through this lens that I find myself looking back at the other mentors and mentorees who have walked alongside me on my journey. So who is this leader who has shaped my thinking about leadership? What elements formed this wise mentor, whose thinking and leadership have been formative in my own understanding of the mentoring process? When we interviewed Max De Pree we identified five characteristics that have shaped his leadership, his life and his mentoring – five elements evocative of the resources that mentors bring to the mentoring relationship.

Chapter 3 looks back over the key persons who walked into my life as mentors, exploring the various forms that mentoring took and what I have learned about mentoring when I look back from the perspective of research and reflection.

Chapters 4 through 7 explore the relationship between mentor and mentoree. Mentors encourage reflection on the character of leadership in intentional, exclusive, intensive, voluntary relationships. What makes a good mentor? What do mentors look for in a mentoree? If mentoring is such an important learning relationship, how do we get started? Where do we begin? What does an effective mentoring relationship look like?

Chapters 8 and 9 reflect on the mentoring relationship with some thoughts about content and technique. The responsibilities of leadership create natural points of tension inherent in the role. Understanding and living with each of these tensions of leadership is critical to our effectiveness as leaders. Mentoring relationships provide the safe context in which to explore these tensions as we work out how we will live and thrive without complete resolution. The tensions of leadership elicit a natural agenda for mentoring discussion. Mentoring is a relationship, an art. It cannot be programmed and I am very cautious about "technique." However, the important role of questions needs to be addressed. Mentoring is more about asking good questions than giving good answers. Questions frame the future of life and leadership. Appropriately, I think, the book ends with questions – matters for further reflection and discussion with your mentors and mentorees. The value of this book will be directly proportional to the number of questions that remain when you put it down.

1. Character

Mentoring reflects on the character of leadership

To get us started, here are three questions for you to think about. I would encourage you to reflect briefly on each question and take the time to write them out. Be honest. There is no trick to this. This is for your benefit, to provoke your thinking. Take your time. Your answers to these questions may be the most important information you ponder while reading this book.

What is the most important thing in life to you?

Projecting yourself forward to the end of your life, what do you want to be known for?

At this stage in your journey, what do you need to learn next?

Okay, why the questions? I believe that, if you were honest, what you wrote down has a direct impact on the productivity of your company, the success of your organization, or the accomplishment of your mission. How you answered the questions touches the bottom line of your organization however you measure the bottom line.

The first question is the question of *character.* Who are you? What values do you bring to your leadership? It begins to get at the passions, the commitments that drive us, that shape the way we relate to people, use our time, and set our priorities. Whatever is most important to us will impact the productivity of our organizations.

When I first suggested this equation to my son, the director of investor relations for a company in Minnesota, he scoffed and said "No way. I wrote down Mary [his fiancée]. What does she have to do with my company?" Then he paused and after some reflection continued a bit sheepishly, "Well, maybe you are right. I'm in Minnesota now. Mary is in California. I route every business trip I take through California and spend a considerable amount of time trying to figure out how to get to California as often as possible. I suppose that does impact the way I do my work here." Exactly. Who we are, what is important to us, and our commitments and passions do shape our leadership, and leadership impacts outcomes.

The second question is the question of *legacy.* What do you want to be known for? It touches on purpose, calling, meaning, and accountability. We travel through life like ships at sea, leaving a wake behind us. We are leaving a legacy as we live, as we work, as we serve in leadership roles. What do you want to be known for? What kind of wake, what kind of legacy do you want to leave? This is a key question for leaders: Who do you intend to be? What legacy will you leave? Because, again, this has a direct impact on the productivity of our organizations. Our sense of calling, of purpose, of meaning will shape the way we relate to people, the way we exercise leadership. Leadership flows from character and it leaves a legacy.

The third question focuses on the *present*: What do you need to learn next? It opens the door to growth, to learning, and, of course, to risk and vulnerability. Growth is always a risky business. Growth – new learning – implies change. It suggests movement into new territory, new ideas. And that leaves us vulnerable. But again, to quote Max De Pree: "We cannot become what we need to be by remaining what we are."[1] This is where mentoring begins – with the answer to the third question. I believe that leaders must continue to grow and that mentors can help facilitate that learning process. When we know what we need to learn next, we look for a mentor to help us learn. In fact, a good mentor is the person with whom we would feel comfortable talking about our answers to all three questions. What is the most important thing in life to you? What do you want to be known for? And at this stage in your leadership journey, what do you want to learn next?

The connection between character and productivity

Before we begin to examine the mentoring process as a leadership development strategy, let me walk through the model that helps me visualize the connection between character, legacy, productivity and mentoring.

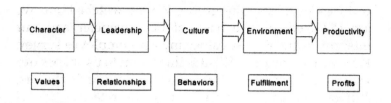

Character

The first box, character, represents what I am getting at with the first question. Character is the mix of commitments, beliefs, passions, and assumptions that forms who we are. Our character defines us and is expressed in the values that we bring to life and leadership.[2] Our character is expressed in our values (that which is important to us): both our stated values and our behaviors (our acted values). Our stated values are those we proclaim in our core value statements, our creeds, and our public commitments. But our true values are always reflected in behaviors and actions.[3] What we really believe always shows up in our actions. And of course this is what integrity is all about. We have integrity when our behaviors are aligned with our stated values.[4] It all starts with character – who we are – because who we are shapes everything we do and everyone we touch.

The importance of character is supported by the research of Kouzes and Posner, reported in their excellent books *The Leadership Challenge* and *Credibility*.[5] The arrow between character and leadership represents this research. The research suggests that people follow people of character, people who are credible. Leadership is a relationship in which the character of the leader elicits the behavior of the followers. The character of the leader shapes leadership because, as Daniel Goleman, the Harvard psychologist notes, leaders are the most watched people in any group. We are watched and we are followed, on the basis of our character and our integrity – the highest values in every employee survey. Who you are matters. What is important to us shapes our values and behaviors. And our values, our behaviors, and our integrity translates into our relationships of leadership.[6]

Leadership

Leadership is a relationship between two persons in which one person seeks to influence the behavior, attitudes, vision, or values of another. It is always a relationship and it always rests in the hands of the followers. It does not matter what our title is or how much authority we think we have. Unless someone chooses to follow, we have not led. In the end, followers determine leadership, and, as Kouzes and Posner report, followers look for integrity.[7] The character of the leader therefore shapes the leadership of the organization; and leadership finds its expression in relationships.

Edgar Schein, the distinguished professor from MIT argues that the only thing of unique importance leaders do is create and reinforce culture.[8] By culture he means the beliefs, values, assumptions, traditions and commitments that are so deeply embedded in the organization that they operate unconsciously – "the way we do things here." Schein's research makes the connection between leadership and culture because everything that leaders do and say reinforces the values embedded in the organizational culture – *everything*. The longer you serve in a leadership role the more the values reflecting your character will be absorbed by and embedded in the culture or character of the organization, even as you will absorb some of the values of the organization.[9]

Culture

Culture controls the behaviors of the people in our organizations. Culture reflects what is really important regardless of the corporate value statements. Culture shapes the way people relate to one another and do their work within the organization. It is revealed in the everyday interactions and behaviors of the people.[10] When the De Pree Center goes in to study an organization, we like to ask employees what they would tell a friend who was just starting to work at their company, what their friend would need to know to thrive there, and what would get them fired. This begins to get at culture. But the best way to see culture in action is to watch the people at work. Their relationships and their work will reflect the corporate values embedded in the culture.

So you can begin to see the connection. Who we are – our character – shapes our leadership. Our leadership creates and reinforces the culture of the organization. Our values, passed on through the relationships of leadership, find expression in the behaviors of the people who work in our companies.[11] If I spend enough time with the people who work for you, I will have a fairly good picture of your character and the values that you bring to your leadership.

Environment

In the book *In Good Company*, Don Cohen and Laurence Prusak show that organizational culture creates the context or environment experienced by the people who work there[12]. Like Daniel Goleman, Cohen and Prusak recognize that leaders set the tone of an organization through their actions, teaching what it takes to succeed in the company. The level of trust that leadership communicates and reinforces within the organization creates the social capital that funds the relationships of the community and ultimately determines the health of the culture. A culture where people experience trust and respect, generous affirmation, and recognition of their personal lives encourages loyalty, continuity and longevity.[13] It is good to work where you are appreciated and respected, where you belong, where people listen and take you seriously. When the character of leadership is expressed with integrity, it nurtures a culture of openness and trust (or conversely secrecy and suspicion), which builds the social connections that make the experience of work positive and productive (or negative and confining). Leadership shapes culture, and that contributes to people finding satisfaction and fulfillment in their work.

Productivity

Of course, healthy environments lead to employee satisfaction. Joe Maciariello, in his study of ServiceMaster, and Daniel Goleman, in his study of primal leadership, both demonstrate that employee satisfaction usually leads to employee retention, which can normally be translated into customer satisfaction, which, in turn, naturally links directly to productivity – mission accomplishment or profits.[14]

It is all connected. Character shapes leadership. Leadership shapes culture. Culture shapes the experience of employees. The experience of employees impacts productivity. The pressures of leadership often narrow the leader's focus to the bottom line. That is one reason why we need mentors. Mentors tend to ask questions that broaden the focus to issues of character and leadership. And that is important to personal growth, to leadership development, to organizational effectiveness, and to productivity. Why? Because it is all connected. Leadership makes a difference; and it is the character of the leader that shapes the relationships of leadership.

Theology

But there is one more box to add to the far left of our chart. In this box I write "Gods," because the gods that we follow shape the person we are. Our character is a reflection of our faith, our beliefs, our commitments, the mentors we learn from, the promises we make, and the gods we follow. This is our theology.

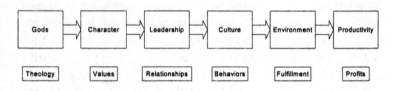

Gods	Character	Leadership	Culture	Environment	Productivity
Theology	Values	Relationships	Behaviors	Fulfillment	Profits

When I add this box with religious leaders, there is a tendency to relax because we know the God we follow. And this is probably true. But remember the connections. If I spend time with the people in your organization, not only will I have a picture of the values that you hold, but I will begin to see the gods you follow. God may be one, but will the behaviors of your people suggest other gods as well?

Theology matters. Eugene Peterson argues in his biblical study of Herod, Caiaphas and Josephus, that whom we choose to follow shapes who we are.[15] The gods we follow form our character. And our character shapes our leadership and reaches the bottom line. Joe Maciariello makes this connection clearly in his study of ServiceMaster. He traces the commitment "To Honor God in All We Do" from the leadership of the company to the bottom line productivity of the organization.[16] Theology matters – because it will show up in the culture of your organization and the in lives of the people who look to you for leadership.

Because theology shows, the three questions with which we began this chapter are important. Leaders teach theology all day long. Jean Lipman-Blumen, a professor at the Drucker Graduate School of Management, argues that people look to leaders to help them understand what is important in life.[17] She understands that everyone is on a journey in life, trying to determine how to live in the face of impending death. Leaders, she argues, offer hope, structure, and direction. People look to leaders to understand what is important. As leaders, we have an amazing opportunity and responsibility to serve – the people who look to us for leadership and the organization that entrusts us with a vision, a mission. This is why I think it is essential that a leader takes time for reflection, time to stop and think: What is important in my life? What values do I bring to my leadership? What theology am I teaching with my leadership? Do my actions and words align? What kind of legacy am I leaving? We need to stop and think about these questions, *because the people who look to us for leadership probably already know the answers.* They are watching and learning from our words and our actions. Max De Pree likes to ask the question: Who do you intend to be? I like to couple that with the question: What would your granddaughter learn about God, life, and work by following you around all day?

I spent a week with my two grandsons recently. Brendon, the older is three. He has entered the "why?" stage of life. "Granddad, why does the wind blow? Why does everyone have to die? Why can't I marry mommy? Why can't I be a nun? Why do I have to go to bed? Why?

Why? Why?" He is watching everything and drawing conclusions. When he asks why, he is on the right track, because leadership is more about asking good questions than giving good answers.

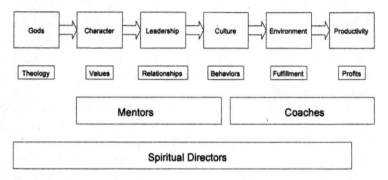

To finish framing this model let me position three kinds of question-askers.

Mentors tend to ask questions that help us reflect on the link between character, leadership, and culture. Executive coaches tend to ask questions that help us think about the applications linking leadership to productivity. Spiritual directors help us see how the gods we follow shape everything else. These are not intended to be tightly defined distinctions. The three roles often overlap with one another and with teachers and counselors. But it helps to position the lens of this book – the mentoring relationship. This is where we will focus. However, I believe that as we walk this journey of leadership from, time to time we need to reflect on the questions posed by all three of these guides.

What is the most important thing in life to you? Who are you? Projecting yourself forward to the end of your life, for what do you want to be known? What legacy are you leaving? At this stage in your journey, what do you need to learn next? Where is your growing edge? I have been asked these questions by various people over the years, but it was Max De Pree who placed them at the heart of the mentoring relationship.

2. Leadership

Leadership reflects the character of the relational leader

From early years I have been privileged to have mentors enter my life and walk alongside for portions of my journey. Several stand out for the significant impact they have had on my life and leadership. But one mentor emerges at the top of my list: Max De Pree. Not only has he been the person with whom I have had the longest mentoring relationship, but also he is the person with whom I have reflected most on the nature of mentoring. Conversations with this mentor have greatly shaped my understanding of relational leadership and the importance of mentoring as a relationship of leadership development, personal renewal, and succession planning.

Max De Pree served for over forty years with the Herman Miller Corporation. He held a variety of positions, leaving his mark most profoundly as CEO and Chairman. During his tenure of leadership, Herman Miller was one of the most respected companies in the United States, continually studied for its people-centered management, its successful innovation and its strong return to its shareholders. His four leadership books – *Leadership is an Art, Leadership Jazz, Leading without Power,* and *Called to Serve* – continue to be bestsellers among the literature of management and leadership. Max is broadly recognized for his relational leadership; but there have been a handful of men and women who have benefited particularly from the gracious wisdom of this leader. Over the years Max De Pree has served as a mentor and friend to a group of younger leaders who looked to him as a model and, as I have noted above, that has been his wonderful gift to me. For over twenty-one years, Max De Pree has been my mentor, my teacher, my coach, and my friend. His steady wisdom followed me through the turmoil of various middle management positions, the successes and struggles of twelve years as President of Regent College, a graduate school affiliated with the University of British Columbia in Canada, and now into a role where I am charged by a board to promote and continue the relational leadership and mentoring legacy of Max De Pree.

A mentor's approach to leadership

In the role I have with the De Pree Leadership Center, I am now looking at Max De Pree through a new lens. For years he was the model of relational leadership for me. His philosophy of management, his theology of leadership formed the framework for my forays into leadership. During my tenure at Regent College I was an administrator, intentionally trying to apply the leadership approach of Max De Pree to a graduate school of Christian studies. However, now I need the perspective of an educator instead of a manager. The De Pree Center seeks to teach people how to be effective relational leaders. Yet after serving more than thirty years in organizational leadership I have learned that leadership cannot be taught. It must be lived. It can be learned but it cannot be explained in a neat package or formula. The best article title on leadership I have seen was called "Leadership as muddling through." That says it all. Leadership is a messy mixture of people, passions, vision, and constraints, pushing and pulling in multiple directions. There is not one way to do it. Not even a right way to do it. It is more a matter of living with vision, character and integrity in the midst of a network of relationships.

Consequently, I have not been very gracious with the many leadership models that have emerged over the years, with their neat steps, principles, habits, rungs, rings, or paths. Occasionally, I would try to put what I was learning into a formula or structure, but it always fell short. I do not believe you can tell someone what to do in a future leadership situation. You have to be present and to act out of your vision and your values with the full vulnerability that you might be wrong. Maybe that's why one of the definitions of leadership I like is: Leadership is the risk of deciding when the alternatives are equal.[1] It does not require leadership to choose when one choice is better. Leadership is the risk of choosing when every choice might be right – or wrong. It is the risk of leading in the midst of ambiguity.

Is there then a definable relational approach to leadership? Can we identify the elements of relational leadership and teach them? Armed with these questions I decided to interview my mentor, Max De Pree. With the help of Dr. Joyce Avedisian, Director of Knowledge Management for Aventis Pharmaceuticals, we structured a day-long interview with Max De Pree to probe his thinking about leadership and relationships. Out of that day five formative elements surfaced that helped us understand one effective leader's approach to relational leadership and opened a continuing conversation about the importance of mentoring. Five themes have governed the leadership development of Max De Pree and they serve as pointers to all of us on the journey of leadership:

- mentors and teachers
- a philosophy or theology of management
- the personal character and integrity of the leader
- learning through mentoring others
- asking questions that define reality

Mentors and teachers

The first theme to emerge in the interview was mentoring. Max De Pree talks about the colonel in his army training who showed him the power of choice and helped him to see that there were often more choices available than those that are first presented. He speaks and writes often of the powerful influence of his father, D. J. De Pree, a man who understood his calling in life to be worked out partly through his role as a leader of people and manufacturer of quality goods. Max found in Carl Frost a brilliant advocate for people, a man who understood organizations, human relationships, and the power of ownership. With Peter Drucker, he established a long-term relationship that mentored and coached him in the management of people and his development as a leader of Herman Miller. And finally, David Hubbard, a life-long friend and spiritual mentor, helped Max reflect on the ethical, moral, and faith dimensions of leadership and life. There is no question in De Pree's mind that who he is today, as a person and as a leader, was formed profoundly by his association with these mentors in his life. *The mentors we choose shape the person we are and the leadership we offer.* Later we will return to this critical theme.

A philosophy or theology of management

In Chapter 1 we noted the role that theology plays in shaping character and leadership. Max De Pree illustrates this well. His theological convictions as a Christian played a role in his leadership development. As Max would say, some truths, once understood, shape the way we look at leadership, people, and organizations. In our conversation with Max, a theology of management began to take shape with broad strokes: the leadership of God, the dignity of persons, the relational nature of life, the diversity of community, the inclusion of the marginalized, and the stewardship of creation.

- *The leadership of God:* Christian thinking about leadership starts with the recognition that God is King – the leader – and all human leadership is exercised in service to God. In the Hebrew Scriptures the kings who looked to God as the nation's leader were successful in their reigns. Those who believed that they were the leaders were destined to fall.[2] From Genesis to Malachi, the message is simple: God is the leader of the people of God. Jesus underlines the same theme as he announces the presence of the Kingdom of God in the Christian Scriptures. All that he does, he does in the name of God, whose Kingdom he brings.[3] God is the King, the one true leader. All other leadership exists in the service of God, the people of God, and the creation of God. Leadership for men and women is always about service, always carried out in the presence of God. Leadership always begins with following. God is the leader.
- *Men and women created in the image of God:* It is impossible to read the writing of Max De Pree without coming face to face with his concept of persons. The biblical truth that human beings are created in the

image of God for relationship with God and have been redeemed by God,[4] suggests leadership starting with the premise that all persons have value, personal worth, and potential to be released and encouraged. People deserve respect as persons created in the image of God; they deserve the space and opportunity to realize their potential before God. Leadership serves this truth, abandoning itself to the strengths of the people for whose success the leader is responsible.

- *The relational nature of life from a Triune God:* Leadership is about relationship because life is about relationship. A faith commitment to a Triune God leads to an understanding of the relational nature of life. Men and women are created for relationship – for relationship with God and for relationship with one another – for community. Leadership is always a relationship. One theology book I return to regularly is L. Gregory Jones' excellent work, *Embodying Forgiveness.* Jones captures well both the dignity of creation and its relational nature.

> The Triune God is characterized by self-giving love; further, God loves those whom God has created. God wills communion with Creation, and so creates human beings in the divine image and likeness. So human beings are created for loving communion – with God, with one another, and with the whole Creation; we are not made to live as isolated or self-enclosed individuals. Hence, we can only fulfill our purpose and destiny when we fulfill our God-given capacity to love, to live as a part of the pattern of God's Creation. In an analogous fashion to God's self-giving life among Father, Son, and Spirit, we find our life in self-giving love with others. The "deepest truth" about ourselves is neither that we are self-sufficient nor that [we] are weak, needy, and fallible; it is that we are created for communion with God, with

one another, and with the whole Creation. We need God and others both to discover who and whose we are and also because it is only through our life together that we can fulfill our destiny for communion in God's Kingdom.[5]

- *The gifted diversity and interdependence of human community:* For one who reads the New Testament it is clear that men and women were created in the image of God for participation in the community of Christ. Each person has been gifted by the Spirit of God to contribute to as well as benefit from his or her engagement in community.[6] This means that we need one another and that everyone has something to offer. Thus, a theology of management embraces diversity and recognizes that each person has worth in himself or herself and is a gift to the community.
- *The inclusiveness of the marginalized:* Biblical community, however, is not just about diversity. The individual worth and contribution of each member is defined in relationship to the body of Christ – the community of persons. Diversity has value only in the context of inclusivity. And that of course is another important theological theme – the inclusiveness of community. Everyone belongs; no one can be marginalized in true community if we take the image of God and diversity seriously.[7] Leaders have a particular responsibility to work for the inclusiveness of those who find themselves on the margins of our communities and organizations.
- *Everyone belongs:* Everyone has something to contribute to a community of people created by God. Robert Fulghum, a minister and author in Seattle, captures this well in his story about the mermaid. Fulghum was leading a group of 80 children in a

romping gymnasium game called Giants, Wizards, and Dwarfs. It is a large-scale version of Rock, Paper, and Scissors, and requires the kids to chose a group at a chaotic moment in the game. Fulghum writes

> The excitement of the chase had reached a critical mass. I yelled out: "You have to decide now which you are – a Giant, a Wizard, or a Dwarf!" While the groups huddled in frenzied, whispered consultation, a tug came at my pants leg. A small child stands there looking up, and asks in a small concerned voice, "Where do the Mermaids stand?"
>
> Where do the Mermaids stand?
>
> A long pause... A very long pause. "Where do the Mermaids stand?" says I.
>
> "Yes. You see, I am a Mermaid."
>
> "There are no such things as Mermaids."
>
> "Oh, yes, I am one!"
>
> She did not relate to being a Giant, a Wizard, or a Dwarf. She knew her category. Mermaid. And was not about to leave the game and go over and stand against the wall where a loser would stand. She intended to participate, wherever Mermaids fit into the scheme of things. Without giving up dignity or identity. She took it for granted that there was a place for Mermaids and I would know just where...
>
> What was my answer at the moment? Every once in a while I say the right thing. "The Mermaid stands right here by the King of the Sea!" says I. (Yes, right here by the King's Fool, I thought to myself.)
>
> So we stood there hand in hand, reviewing the troops of Wizards and Giants and Dwarfs as they roiled by in wild disarray.
>
> It is not true, by the way, that mermaids do not exist. I know at least one personally. I have held her hand.[8]

A management philosophy grounded on a biblical concept of persons takes seriously the inclusion of every member as a participating contributor to the organization.

• *The stewardship of creation:* Men and women have been placed in a world created by God. Just as we are defined by our relationship with God and our community of relationships with others, so we are shaped individually and corporately by our relationship with creation. We are stewards. of our environment, entrusted with its care, use, and preservation. Our environment has parallels to community. It is a place where we belong, where we benefit – drawing our sustenance – and where we contribute to its care and sustenance and thereby the care and sustenance of others. We are stewards of our environment.

The personal character and integrity of the leader

Character and integrity, however, require more than just an assent to theological truth or an attachment to mentors and teachers. The leader's touch must match his or her voice.

In his book *Leadership Jazz*, Max tells the poignant story of the birth of his granddaughter.

Esther, my wife, and I have a granddaughter named Zoë, the Greek word for "life." She was born prematurely and weighed one pound, seven ounces, so small that my wedding ring could slide up her arm to her shoulder. The neonatologist who first examined her told us that she had a 5 to 10 percent chance of living three days. When Esther and I scrubbed up for our first visit and saw Zoë in her isolette in the neonatal intensive care unit, she had two IVs in her navel, one in her foot, a monitor on each side of her chest, and a respirator tube and a feeding tube in her mouth.

To complicate matters, Zoë's biological father had jumped ship the month before Zoë was born. Realizing this, a wise and caring nurse named Ruth gave me my instructions. "For the next several months, at least, you're the surrogate father. I want you to come to the hospital every day to visit Zoë, and when you come, I would like you to rub her body and her legs and arms with the tip of your finger. While you're caressing her, you should tell her over and over how much you love her, because she has to be able to connect your voice to your touch."

Ruth was doing exactly the right thing on Zoë's behalf (and, of course, on my behalf as well), and without realizing it she was giving me one of the best possible descriptions of the work of a leader. At the core of becoming a leader is the need always to connect one's voice and one's touch.[9]

Zoë is now a growing young girl. Her ongoing relationship to her grandfather is captured passionately in the little book by Max DePree called *Letters to Zoë*. Many lives have been impacted forever by the values of a man who loved a little girl.

The beliefs, values and commitments of a leader must be lived out in the behaviors of life and the actions of leadership. As we noted in the first chapter, leadership flows from character. Who we are shapes what we do. What we believe matters. The critical issue, however, is to determine that who we *say* we are and what we *say* we believe – our voice – is in fact what is reflected in our behavior – our touch. Integrity is the alignment of voice and touch, the consistent living out of our character intentionally and openly, seeking to become the person we purpose to be. Personal character is defined by our theology – the 'gods' we choose to follow – and therefore our leadership actions flow from our incarnated theological commitments. Who we are matters. What we believe matters. The actions of leadership will always flow from our character. Integrity brings character, voice and touch into the same space.

Learning through mentoring others

The fourth element in this profile of a leader takes us back to the first. Just as Max De Pree sought mentors and teachers to follow in his own leadership development, he has continued this process by offering himself as a mentor and teacher of others. I am only one person who has benefited from this. Clearly, mentoring is a key factor in the leadership of Max De Pree. He was mentored and he continues to mentor others. Partly, this comes naturally, acting out a model that was beneficial to him. But partly, I believe, it is a way that he *continues to learn*. Just as teachers claim to learn more than students do, mentors can learn from the people they mentor. The exploration and articulation of beliefs with another person renews our own thinking and challenges our actions.

Recently the De Pree Center convened a consultation of eight of the persons whom Max De Pree has mentored over the last two decades. It was a wonderful day, as each of us told the story of our relationship with Max. We came from leadership positions in varied organizations – church, non-profit and corporate – and we were a group with diverse personalities and settings. But all of us know that we have been in an empowering relationship with a man who respected us, cared for us, and learned with us about life and leadership. It is a group that plans to continue to meet to encourage the mentoring legacy of Max De Pree.

Asking questions that define reality

In 1993, Ernest Gaines, published an award winning novel called *A Lesson Before Dying*. In this novel, later made into a movie, Gaines sets forth a realistic picture of life in the rural south of the United States in the 1940s. The story focuses on the relationship between two men: Grant and Jefferson. Grant is the local school teacher. Jefferson is a 21-year-old, poor, nearly illiterate, black plantation worker. Jefferson is in prison. He is the only surviving (and maybe innocent) participant in a liquor store hold up that resulted in the death of the owner and two of Jefferson's friends. The store owner was white. Slavery was now illegal, but segregation was the law and Jefferson was easily convicted by the all white jury.

It is Grant's job to teach Jefferson who he is and how to live before the State of Louisiana executes him for murder. As the story unfolds, a small community of people – black and white – face three questions: Who am I? Who cares? And how do I live before I die?

Those are the questions of life. They shape the agenda of leadership. They define the work of mentoring. The questions are about us. But the answers define the reality in which we live and work and exercise leadership.

It is not surprising that questions play such a significant role in leading and mentoring. One of Max De Pree's most quoted statements is: "The first responsibility of a leader is to define reality."[10] Reality is defined by the questions we ask. Max loves to ask questions: Who do you intend to be? What promises are you making? What are you teaching? What are you learning? What legacy do you want to leave? Often I have heard him say that leadership is not about good answers; it is about good questions. Board leadership is about asking questions. Mentoring is about asking questions.

When I think about the relational leadership that I have learned from Max De Pree, I see a string of questions.

Who are you?
    Character: What shapes you?
    Charisma: To what are you committed?

Who cares?
    Connections: To whom are you committed?
    Culture: What are you reinforcing?

What legacy are you leaving?
    Community: What are you building?
    Contribution: What do you measure?

These are the questions that define reality. They are the questions of relational leadership. They are the work of mentoring.

Conclusion

Mentors and teachers, a philosophy of management, integrity of character, mentoring others, and asking questions: These five elements appear as reoccurring themes in the writings of Max De Pree and in his talks and conversations. And through them all runs a deep commitment to relationships – first with God, then with mentors – because, again, whom you choose to follow forms your character and shapes your relationships with the people you lead. Leadership reflects the character of the relational leader. At the heart of relational leadership lies a passion for relationships and mentoring – choosing to invest oneself in the life and leadership of another. This is the legacy of leadership. And reflection on this legacy leads me to ponder the presence of other mentors on my journey.

3. Encouragement

Mentoring shapes the character of relational leadership

My introduction to mentoring

Don Bubna, fresh from his theological training, was the pastor of a small church north of San Diego. It was his first church. He was young, but he cared about the people in his congregation. He took time to learn from the elders of his community – the long-time members. He visited homes and hospitals, dropped in for coffee with families.

As he got to know his people better, he chose a tall, shy teenager and invited him to the donut shop. This was the beginning of a long friendship and an intentional mentoring relationship. He affirmed and encouraged the youth, meeting him every Wednesday after school. I was that 14-year-old boy, and Donald Bubna was the first of several mentors who would shape my life.

I did not know it then, but now, forty-seven years later, I recognize what was happening. I was being mentored. And for the past forty-seven years, mentors have played important roles in my life and have taught me how to give this gift to others. For some reason Don Bubna took an interest in me. Every Wednesday he met me at the donut shop after school. He listened to me, encouraged me, believed in me. I don't know if he taught me any-thing specific or was directive in his mentoring; I only know that he believed in me at a time when my confidence was low. Under his mentoring I moved into leadership roles in the church youth program.

We did not talk about this as a mentoring relationship. In fact, I am not sure I even knew what a mentor was at the time. He did not present himself as my mentor, and I was not seeking or following a mentor. But now looking back it is clear to me that this was my first formal mentoring relationship beyond parents and teachers – an older and wiser person affirming and encouraging my journey.

This relationship continued in some form through my first year of college, during which time he helped me think through my life purposes and calling, and encouraged my transfer from a large state university to a small, private college in San Francisco. The move to San Francisco was the end of our regular mentoring sessions but not the end of the relationship. Don Bubna kept track of my wanderings through graduate study in Scotland and California, and through various management res-ponsibilities over the years. I believe there is an im-portant truth about mentoring illustrated here. Mentor-ing is intentional and focused. Relationships are larger and looser. Don Bubna and I have remained friends and sustained a relationship over the past forty-seven years as our lives intersected from time to time. But the mentoring phase of our relationship embraced the five years of my life from ages 14 to 19. For five critical years of my journey, Don Bubna walked alongside and helped me think about the path I would choose to walk.

Don saw potential and invested himself in me. In him I saw someone who believed in me, affirmed me, and encouraged me. And I found the confidence to live up to his confidence. *Mentors recognize and affirm potential.* This may be the heart of the mentoring relationship.

For me, as I look back over the gift of mentors in my life, *the formal mentoring relationship is an intentional, exclusive, intensive, voluntary relationship between two persons.* It is a relationship – a teaching/learning connection between two persons – in which both persons work to nurture the relationship – to contribute to the connection.

Others define mentoring more broadly. Some approach the topic with a focus on mentors as any person of influence in the lives of others. With this broader definition, mentoring would occur with or without an intentional relationship. Anyone whose words or actions shape the way we think and live is a mentor. Thus, mentors could be close or distant, alive or dead. We all continue to learn from the words and reported actions of people we have never met; they continue to teach us and shape our lives. And, of course, this perspective reminds us that even without our knowledge people may be looking to us as models and learning something about living by watching our lives. Everyone teaches what is important by the way they live their lives. I do believe there is a kind of teaching happening when we intentionally seek to learn from the journey of another even if they are unaware of our learning. But this is not a mentoring relationship. In relationships learning goes both ways. Similarly, I do not believe that mentoring occurs every time someone comes alongside to affirm and encourage. An intentional mentor without an engaged learner is not a mentoring relationship.

In this book I will use the term 'mentor' to designate intentional, exclusive, intensive, voluntary relationships between two persons, usually with the intent to grow and develop one of the persons toward an agreed upon goal or objective. And like all relationships, even though the purpose will be to grow one person, the process of relationship building allows both persons to give and to receive, to teach and to learn. Mentoring is a dance of teaching and learning together.

Mentors offer a safe place to gain perspective

When I began my college studies in San Francisco, I was assigned an academic advisor. I still did not understand the role of mentors – but Roland Given became one. He met with each of his advisees, listened to us, believed in us, encouraged us, and helped us think through decisions during a formative time in our lives. Under Roland Given's watchful encouragement, I engaged in campus politics and began to learn about leadership. He guided my academic program and nudged me along the path to graduate school. He also brought us into his life and family. I remember eating at the Given home and babysitting for their three small sons. I do not remember much of the content of our relationship, but I remember the affirmation and the encouragement to pursue graduate study. He believed I could do it. Again my life was shaped.

As I look back over my experience with Roland Given, it is clear to me that mentors may give advice when asked, but much more importantly they give blessing and encouragement to risk learning and growth. By listening and giving honest feedback in safe trusted conversation, the mentor both affirms the perspective of the mentoree and broadens it gently. Through this affirmation and encouragement, mentors like Roland Given encourage self-reliance and confidence. By creating a safe environment for the relationship, the mentor enables the mentoree to step out of the comfort zone and risk something new or untried. Most of us do not want to fail, but it is a gift to be in a relationship that encourages risk and promises to be there to bring learning out of failure.

Reflect again on the image of the mountaineering rope described in the introduction. When I am roped to a stronger experienced climber, it is easier to risk the next move, to stretch for the next foot- or handhold, knowing that if I fall, I will not fall far before the other person on the rope will stop my fall and hold me safely while I find my footing again. It may be easier but it still requires a high level of trust. I have balanced with trembling legs on small ledges resisting the encouragement of my partner to reach for the next crack in the rock. Stretching and succeeding is personally rewarding and brings more affirmation and encouragement. But I am convinced that the value of the rope and the relationship is not really experienced until you miss the mark you were reaching for and fall. Until you fall at least once and feel the security of the rope and the strength of your climbing partner, fear can prevent you from risking the next move. When you feel the security of the rope you are energized to climb, to take the risk. The rope, the relationship, the guide, the mentor create the safe space to risk the next step. *Mentors provide a safe place to regain perspective and energy.*

Mentors bring strengths and weaknesses to the relationship

I entered graduate school thinking I was called to be a pastor – like Don Bubna. And then I met George Ladd, a crusty old professor of New Testament Theology. Dr. Ladd became my first formal mentor in the academic sense of that term. In his classes I caught a passion for life, community, relationships, eternal values and a vision for lifelong learning. I became a student of biblical theology and George Ladd became my doctoral mentor.

He intimidated me and pushed me. He argued with my ideas and let me know how little I knew, but he also showed me the beauty of truth and fed my appetite for study. My calling in life began to shift toward the academy. I wanted to learn and teach.

But George Ladd also taught me about humanness, vulnerability, and the pain of life. We played handball each week and talked. I began to know a brilliant man struggling with life – a man lonely and uncertain about his legacy – a man who taught about community but found relationships difficult to sustain. He shaped forever my vision of life as community, relationships, and character, but he was not a happy man himself. I began to realize that mentors do not necessarily have it all together. They also are in the process of learning and growing. They too are on a journey. But they can still believe in you and share something of themselves with you as you walk together on your journeys.

This was an important lesson for me. Mentors are people too. We choose them because of their perceived maturity, wisdom, and experience. However, mentors, like all other human beings, bring their complete selves to the relationship – their strengths and their weaknesses. To the extent that mentors understand their weaknesses, it can be a touch point for learning and an arena of growth for both persons. To the extent that mentors do not recognize their weaknesses there is potential for damage. When mentors put their insecurities, weaknesses, and fears on the table for discussion, the modeled vulnerability opens doors for learning and growth in two ways. First, the mentoree has opportunity to learn about vulnerability, honesty, and truth. Everyone has strengths and weaknesses, fear as well as courage. Too often on our journey we present a face to the world that belies the turmoil that goes on within, the uncertainties and questions that swirl in our minds. When we can face our fears and articulate our questions, we open the potential for growth and learning. Mentors we respect, who take us into the struggles of their journey, give us hope through their progress and model a courage from which we can learn. We walk our journey in strength and weakness, learning from and building on both. But second, the mentoree needs to cultivate the independent objectivity to choose different paths from the mentor. In every mentoring relationship, while there is always the overwhelming respect that makes the mentor attractive, there will normally be decisions, behaviors, and beliefs of the mentor that the one being mentored may choose not to adopt. Mentoring is not a cloning process. It is intended to develop the unique person of the mentoree, and that requires a differentiation from the mentor.

Mentors, however, who are blind to their own weaknesses, prejudices, or insecurities can be a risk. A core purpose of the mentoring process is to assist mentorees to develop accurate self-awareness, self-understanding, and self-control as they choose their path in life. A mentor without accurate self-awareness or self-understanding may provide distorted encouragement or direction to those being mentored. I have watched gifted leaders offer their services as mentors, seemingly unaware of what others perceive as an attempt to control a younger leader either by direction or by association. Most of us live and act with mixed motivations. Effective mentors work hard to be clear about the good and bad motives that shape their behaviors. And of course because the mentoring relationship is committed to both persons realizing their potential, it might provide the context in which the mentor through the articulation of his or her own values and choices may find perspective, learning, and growth. *Mentoring is a relationship between fallible human beings and cannot exist without forgiveness and grace.*

Mentors find joy in the progress of mentorees

During my doctoral studies our second son was born and I needed to work. Cal Schoonhoven took a chance on me and defined my life direction. Dr. Schoonhoven had just been appointed special Assistant to the President for Academic Affairs, and he needed an administrative assistant; for some reason he chose me.

Technically, Cal Schoonhoven was an employer – a supervisor – but he also filled the role of mentor. He had administrative responsibilities and he delegated major assignments to me – assignments that I had no idea how to do. Yet he believed in me, encouraged me, and trusted me to figure out what I needed to know. And he affirmed my efforts. From this relationship I learned the value of lavish affirmation. I received so much affirmation from Cal Schoonhoven that I was eager to learn what I needed to know to take on the next responsibility. It was easy to risk venturing into new arenas with such an affirming coach at my side. Under his encouraging guidance I realized that I actually enjoyed the administrative side of education – something most academics prefer to avoid – and a new tangent was taken in the trajectory of my development.

Mentors can see leadership potential, often before we see it in ourselves. With encouragement and affirmation they can nurture the gifts and calling to service that finds expression in leadership. Not all employee-manager relationships are mentoring relationships, but the manager is well placed to mentor those in the organiza-tion with the potential for leadership. I believe this is the heart and the promise of relational leadership. It is particularly important for succession planning and leadership transition within organizations.

Cal Schoonhoven was my manager and mentor. Again, we did not use the language of mentoring, but I believe he was intentionally encouraging my development in leadership and I knew that he was giving me wonderful opportunities to learn with lavish encouragement to risk that growth. And there was a selfless side to Schoonhoven's mentoring role. When the arena of academic administration expanded, Dr. Schoonhoven put me forward for increased responsibilities, preferring to maintain his own faculty leadership in the library. It was not long before I found myself serving on the President's staff in academic research and planning. Again, someone believed in me, identified abilities that had not yet been developed, provided opportunity for growth, encouraged my efforts, and lavishly affirmed my progress. I still trace the beginning of my journey in organizational leadership back to the time I spent with Calvin Schoonhoven.

Mentors share their hopes and dreams

But if Cal Schoonhoven launched my journey of leadership, Glenn Barker shaped it. For twelve years I had the gift of Glenn Barker teaching me what servant leadership was all about. When he was appointed Dean and subsequently Provost, he took me on as mentoree, protégé, or as he liked to say "alter ego." He was my organizational supervisor – the corporate Vice President for the institution. But he was much more than that. From the day of our first meeting, Glenn Barker established the parameters of our relationship. He was a verbal person – a college debater – and he needed to think out loud, to talk his ideas through. He wanted a safe relationship in which to think, and he took me into his head and his heart. We talked about everything – his vision and passion for the institution, his hopes, dreams, plans, and frustrations, theology, family, life, and relationships. For twelve years I was privileged to walk with a gifted successful relational leader. Everything he did, every decision he made, everything he believed and valued was on the agenda for discussion – the ups and downs, the successes and failures. What an opportunity for learning!

Glenn Barker had a passion for relational leadership and organizational community. Years later I remember telling someone whom I was mentoring that I was not sure if Glenn Barker changed the institution as much as he would have liked, but he changed me for ever. I cannot think about servant leadership, relational leadership, and organizational community without remembering the model of Glenn Barker. And, as my wife Beverly and anyone who has worked with me can attest, I learned well the need to think out loud about everything. Glenn Barker died of a heart attack while he was my mentor, but his legacy lives on in every leadership responsibility I accept. Like the others, he believed in me, encouraged me and affirmed me. But more than anyone else, he trusted me with his hopes and dreams and visions. *Mentors open their hearts and minds and share themselves.*

Managers can be mentors

Some people would call Glenn Barker's leadership approach coaching – this way of walking alongside someone, caring about them, getting them involved, and engaging them fully in the task at hand – this sharing of yourself, your experience and your wisdom.[1] I believe there is a definite connection between mentoring and the executive coaching or leadership development that has become popular in leadership circles. In many ways executive coaching is a professional form of mentoring – an intentional, exclusive, intensive, voluntary relationship – but it is also usually a contractually defined relationship within an organizational setting focused on specific skill development.[2]

As Glenn Barker taught me, mentoring is a personal relationship that shapes the values of the mentoree by direct teaching and by indirect modeling. Over the years, I have come to believe strongly that such a relationship can exist simultaneously with an organizationally defined relationship. Yet mentoring that occurs within an organizational context brings particular strengths and concerns to the relationship. A mentor within the organization can help the mentoree fit and belong in the organization and develop ownership for the mission and outcomes. There is a danger, however, of the relationship becoming too attached. The mentor cannot always expect the mentoree to rally to his or her organizational agenda. Just as in personal life and values, the mentoree needs to be able to differentiate from the agenda of the mentor. On the other hand, if the mentor is seen as the protective champion of the mentoree, there is the risk that once the mentor is gone, the mentoree will need to leave as well.

With those caveats, however, I do believe it is possible for organizational leaders to serve as mentors for persons for whose success they are responsible. In fact, I believe mentoring is the heart and promise of relational leadership. The proximity, the knowledge of the shared mission and the accumulated wisdom of the organization have much to offer the mentoring relationship. But the question always arises: How safe is this relationship? It is one thing to sustain a mentoring relationship when the organization is thriving. It becomes much more complicated when times are tough and positions are being eliminated.

While organizational constraints must be faced honestly, I do not believe that tough times need to bring the end of the mentoring relationship. Pain, hurt, and disagreement run in the bloodstream of any relationship. The critical elements necessary to sustain the relationship are honesty, objectivity, and trust. Even a painful time of reorganization can be an important time for learning and growth when trust is the dominant force experienced. Both parties in the mentoring relationship need to recognize and acknowledge the various forces working on each of them and the relationship. The mentoring relationship cannot confer special organizational favor on the one being mentored, but it also should not be detrimental to the organizational success of the person. If the organizational pressures become too personal or painful, it may be necessary to suspend the mentoring relationship until the organizational dynamics are resolved. It would be ideal if the relationship could ride through the storm and serve as a learning center for both persons. Only truth, honesty, and trust allow hope for this ideal.

Not every manager can be a mentor to the persons for whose success he or she is responsible. Not every employee wants to be mentored. The manager–employee relationship is its own particular leadership relationship with certain contractual expectations. Within or alongside this relationship, however, when the fit is right and both parties are willing, I believe it is possible to build a deeply meaningful covenantal mentoring relationship. A good mentoring relationship will always seek to be open and honest enough to acknowledge the terms of the organizational relationship.

Mentoring focuses on the one being mentored

Watching the mentors in my life I have learned that mentoring is about mentors sharing themselves with someone to whose growth and success they are committed. It is an investment of the mentor's very self, a sharing of his or her values. It is not a cloning process – not even the cloning of the mentor's values. The focus of mentoring relationships should always be on the one being mentored. The objective of the relationship is the growth and maturity of the mentoree into realization of his or her potential. Mentors provide lavish affirmation and encouragement. They nurture self-learning on the part of the mentoree. Mentors create safe space and provide feedback, share themselves, and offer perspective so that the mentorees can become the persons they choose to be. *Mentoring is not about the mentor. It is always about the one being mentored.* It is not about replicating the mentor. It is always about encouraging the growth of the one being mentored. It is a gift.

An exercise in reflection

As you read this chapter, I hope your mind wandered off occasionally along your own journey. I hope faces emerged in memory of men and women who joined your path and walked with you for a portion of your journey; men and women who served as mentors for your learning and development. The list of men above is the direct result of this kind of reflection. While we were interviewing Max De Pree about the role of mentoring in his leadership development, it became clear that I was one of the long-term mentorees in his story. As we talked I was reminded that Max was not the only person to assume this role in my life. That caused me to stop and reflect. Names emerged. As I continue to lead workshops and teach about mentoring, I am often surprised by new names coming back to mind. My life has been graced with a rich network of mentors and friends.

Before reading further, I would encourage you to stop for such a time of reflection. On a sheet of paper draw a timeline from your birth to the present. On the timeline put a mark at the appropriate place and write above it the major events of history that have occurred during your life. Add the major events of your own story – events or decisions that have shaped your journey to date. Warren Bennis, in his book *Geeks and Geezers*, reminds us that often our lives are shaped strongly by world events or family events outside of our control. He illustrates this with the impact of World War II on his generation compared to the technology revolution shaping his mentorees today.[3] Our stories have context. Our timelines are only single strands in a much larger woven world. There is value in comparing timeline events between mentor and mentoree as we seek understanding of one another and explore how we can learn from our experiences.

On the same timeline make marks at the appropriate dates and write below the line the names of the men and women who have walked portions of your journey alongside you. Were they mentors? Was there an intentional learning relationship? Were they models? Who are the people who have shaped the person you have become to date? As you reflect on these names, can you identify specific things that you learned from them, decisions that you took because of their influence?

We did not always call it mentoring, but most of us can remember a key person or two whose legacy still remains on our life. Everyone deserves to be chosen by mentors.

4. Choice

Mentoring reflects the character of relational leadership

As I continued to grow and accept broader leadership responsibilities, I realized how much I still had to learn. Recognizing how important mentors were, I began to look for them. If Glenn Barker defined relational leadership for me, Max De Pree refined my vision of the leader's legacy. I had heard Max De Pree speak and I read his book. He was the chairman of the board at the institution where I worked. He deeply impressed me with the visible integrity of his life and leadership. Max De Pree was someone I wanted to be near to and learn from. To the extent that I understood them, the values and commitments of Max De Pree were the values and beliefs I brought to leadership. I knew I could learn from him.

Are values enough to make a good mentor? What makes a good mentor?

The elements or ingredients that make a good mentor may differ from person to person and perhaps will even change over the timeframe of one's life. As we move through our own life journey we may look for different experiences or perspectives in a mentor. Effective mentors know when to listen and when to talk. They may bring a network of resources. They are respected broadly and they encourage those around them. At the core, however, I believe there are certain characteristics that I would always seek in a prospective mentor: wisdom, strength of character, shared values, accumulated experiences, continued learning, reflective articulation on life, and accessibility. Each of these elements is important, but it is the character of the person that finally attracts me.

Mentors provide reflective space

A little over twenty-two years ago, I took the audacious step to write to Max De Pree and request a mentoring relationship for two years as part of an educational leadership grant I anticipated receiving. To my surprise and pleasure, he agreed. And then to my surprise and displeasure, I did not get the anticipated grant. I wrote back to Max De Pree, thanked him and informed him that my program was not approved. But I underestimated the generosity of the man. He responded with encouragement and affirmation, and suggested that we start the relationship anyway. That was twenty-two years ago – another gift.

In my initial approach I asked Max to tutor me in leadership, to serve as my mentor for two years. He responded with welcoming enthusiasm but gently resisted the term "mentor." Instead he proposed that he might be a member of my secretariat or board of advisors – a resource person. At that time, for both of us "mentor" sounded too formal, too one-sided. He did not want to accept responsibility for my learning and I was not looking for another professor in my life. Max proposed that he make himself available as a resource, leaving me responsibility to draw on that resource as needed and to seek out other persons with whom to learn as well. He offered a reflective relationship. Thus began the relationship that has helped define mentoring for both of us.

For twenty-two years Max De Pree has been available to me three or four times a year to think with, talk with, weep with, and learn from as I have struggled to understand this journey of leadership. We meet for three to four hours each time, usually over lunch. These have been valuable times for me. He has believed in me, encouraged me, affirmed me, and gently challenged me. During the twelve years I served as President of Regent College, a graduate school affiliated with the University of British Columbia in Canada, Max De Pree was the one with whom I shared my excitement and my frustrations. I usually came away from a meeting with Max with a broader perspective on the reality in which I lived and a renewed sense of hope as I continued to live out my leadership responsibilities. He has been a tremendously formative force in my leadership development. Whether he likes it or not, I am part of the leadership legacy of Max De Pree.

Mentors provide the gift of sanctuary – the opportunity to withdraw from the pressure of daily work and life and reflect on what is happening.[1] In this reflective relationship the mentoree slows down, reviews life's journey and nurtures the self-knowledge that is important to growth. Max De Pree has given that to me. I know that Max serves as a mentor to several other persons, who also value this reflective relationship. And I know from these years that he comes to the role of mentor as one who has experienced and benefited deeply from the mentors who created space for learning in his life. Key men and women were available as resources to Max during his development as a leader. Thus, he understands the value of mentors and makes himself available as a resource to create reflective space for others.

Mentors provide perspective and wisdom

The primary template for my understanding of mentoring is formed by my long-term relationship with Max De Pree. It is also the model that I suggest when others ask me to walk with them as a reflective resource. But this is only one model. My search for mentors and guides along my journey has led me to variations for specific times or purposes.

Sam is a successful business leader working in international commodities trading. The world in which he lives and the pace of life with which he operates are radically different from mine. But Sam comes to his work with some of the same values and passions that I share. He brings to his work a deeply honed character and commitment to service. I do not think of Sam as a place of sanctuary, a person with whom I will have a leisurely reflective relationship. He moves too fast. When we meet in his office, he has one eye on our conversation and one eye on the stock market report. A four-hour conversation over lunch is not the appropriate model. But I know that Sam believes in my potential and is committed to my success. He also has at his fingertips a wealth of information about what is going on in this world and a ready interpretation of trends and possibilities. He has a perspective on life that I need to understand. The model that allows me to benefit most from Sam's wisdom is a short visit or a short telephone call. Sam will ask questions, give feedback, and offer advice as appropriate. But I can hardly keep up when I ask him to tell me what he sees happening in the world this week. His informed perspective and critical analysis challenges my thinking and broadens my understanding of the reality in which I live and serve and provide leadership. The relationship is focused, intentional, and directed toward expanding my perspective. While he might not be comfortable with the term mentor, I think of Sam as a continuing mentor in my life.

Mentors critique ideas and provoke thinking

When I was a graduate student I had academic mentors to challenge my assumptions and stretch my thinking – persons whose job it was to keep me intellectually honest and curious about learning. Once we move into responsibilities of leadership, such feedback is often difficult to find. People do not readily argue with the leader. They are reluctant to point out our inconsistencies and tenuous assumptions. Yet who, more than leaders –who presume to point the direction, whose very words and actions shape the culture and work experience of people – needs such critique?

Jean is an academic, a widely read author and sought after consultant, an expert in the field of leadership with a passion for relational connective leadership. I was first introduced to Jean after accepting my current role directing the De Pree Leadership Center. We are seeking to build a connective organization – a center that exists primarily as a network of interdependent relationships. This is Jean's field of study; she wrote the book on connective leadership. So I called and asked to meet her. Out of that initial conversation a delightful relationship has developed. Jean joined the board of the De Pree Center and makes herself available as a resource mentor for me. While I am not sure she would use the term "mentor" to describe our relationship, that is very much how I see it. In addition to her important contribution to the board, I try to meet with Jean two or three times each year to talk about leadership. She is generous in her encouragement and critical in her thinking. She is a person with whom I can test my developing thoughts on relational leadership and a scholar whose critical questions refresh my perspective. I seldom leave Jean without awareness that there is another avenue of thinking I need to explore. This makes a valuable mentoring relationship.

Mentors learn together in a commitment of trust

Max De Pree thought consciously about including a theologian among his mentors to help him think about ultimate perspectives. I did not – perhaps because I had so many friends with theological education – but it happened anyway. John Bray was the pastor of the church I attended. Dr. Bray was a brilliant thinker and speaker, with specialization in the field of history. When he moved to town we established a relationship that lasted more than eight years. Every Wednesday, John Bray and I would meet at Ernie Jr.'s Taco House for lunch. We did not think we were mentors or mentoring one another, but we needed a safe place to think and talk and argue about life, relationships, community, and leadership – John as pastor/theologian, me as manager/ teacher. We sharpened each other's thinking and enriched each other's spirit. This, I believe, is another piece of mentoring reality – mutual mentoring. *Mentoring is a partnership of learning and encouragement in a commitment of trust*. Just as it can happen within an organizational relationship, mentoring relationships can thrive among peers.

Peer mentors are those friends who know each other well and like one another anyway! They are persons with high trust relationships that care enough to disagree with one another, to call each other to account when their actions do not match their words, to share what they are learning – good and bad. Peer mentoring, like all other mentoring relationships, requires a good fit, a high level of transparency and trust, and probably an interest in common that binds the relationship. But peer mentoring is more than just friendship. It is intentional. It is a deliberate commitment on the part of two friends to hold each other accountable for learning and growth, even as they enjoy one another's company as friends.[2]

Mentors challenge assumptions and uncover theology

I did seek out one other mentor who could give me the broader perspective of theology and spirit as it is worked out in leadership: David Hubbard. After he retired from Fuller Seminary, while I was still President of Regent College, I asked for regular times to meet with him and get his perspective on leadership – particularly in the academy. I had known David Hubbard for years, worked on his staff, and observed his leadership from a safe distance. While he was president, I found it difficult to get close enough for a mentoring relationship, but after his retirement I found a relaxed resource with wisdom abounding, ready to embrace a colleague president with encouragement and thoughtful perspective. In the short time between his retirement and his sudden death, I was privileged to talk with and learn from a wise leader who had successfully lead a premiere faculty of scholars, students, and staff for over thirty years. He realized that everything leaders do and say demonstrates what they really believe – the theology that shapes their character. Our time together often centered on the key question: What are we teaching in our leadership? As a leader who thought theologically about everything he did, David Hubbard set a standard against which leaders would do well to measure themselves. His untimely death placed a marvelous mentor out of reach.

Mentors are not always a good fit

Not all of the mentors I have chosen or been assigned to have worked out. Occasionally, the match was not appropriate. Good people and effective leaders may or may not be the right companion for a particular leg of our journey. Three instances come to mind along my path.

At one point during my leadership development I was assigned a mentor to monitor and encourage my growth as a leader for a period of time. The person was a successful leader, well respected by many in the community, and recognized as an encourager of people. We met at regular intervals, and initially I was impressed by his generous care for me and my work and his desire to walk with me as I learned. However, it was not long into the relationship before I realized that he was more interested in controlling my choices than nurturing my potential. We discussed this perception, but the relationship deteriorated. Long before the assigned time was over, I had ceased to consider him a mentor and took little initiative in setting up meetings.

Later in my leadership journey I met a successful businessman, whose perceptive questions provoked my thinking and offered valuable insights into areas in which I needed to grow. Challenged by his forthrightness, I asked if he would consider a mentoring relationship with me. He was reluctant, and asked for time to ponder my request. Eventually, he agreed, noting that he did not really think he would be a good mentor. However, out of respect for me and my work he would make himself available. He was highly successful in his work, a man of deep character, and generous in his encouragement. After two or three meetings, I concluded that his leadership style took a different tack from the path I was pursing and I was not sure how helpful he would be to my continued growth and development. He affirmed me and my work, but did not encourage the relational style of leadership that I wanted to develop.

My third illustration highlights a different problem. He was a businessman with energy, passion and integrity – a highly successful leader with vision and wisdom to spare, who reflected deeply on every aspect of his role. Whenever I spent time with him I came away stimulated and affirmed, encouraged to take the risks inherent in the responsibilities of leadership. Once again, I proposed a mentoring relationship and he agreed. Unfortunately his willingness to engage in this learning relationship did not translate into the scheduling of his time. It was very difficult to arrange a meeting with him. He did not return telephone calls or email correspondence. He was not accessible. His heart was right and he possessed nearly all of the qualities that make a good mentor. But he lacked one critical element noted by Max De Pree in the Foreword of this book: accessibility. If I could not reach him when I needed to talk, to engage with him on an issue I was struggling with, he could not be an effective mentor. We have remained friends over the years, and I still find my times with him energizing and encouraging, but I do not consider him a mentor. We do not share a mutual commitment to nurturing the learning relationship as a priority in both of our lives.

Having identified these three cases where I did not establish successful mentoring relationships, I want to add a note of caution and humility. There is always something that can be learned from any person walking on this journey of life and leadership. Even when we disagree with their choices, we can learn and choose our own way. The very disagreement can spur us to consider blind spots or strengthen our convictions. To dismiss someone as a potential mentor is as audacious as asking someone to be a mentor. We learn from every relationship. So I am cautious about discounting anyone as a possible mentor. However, we only have so much time to invest in mentoring relationships and we need to choose them with care and intention. The mentoring relationship is a focused working relationship designed for a particular stage of our journey. In the three cases above, I determined that for three different reasons the persons were not appropriate mentors for me at that time in my life and I backed away. In most cases friendship continues but not a mentoring relationship – there is a difference that we will explore more fully in the next chapter.

Mentors offer specific knowledge and expertise

Two of the mentors I noted in Chapter 3, Cal Schoonhoven and Glenn Barker, were my organizational supervisors – managers responsible for my success and growth. While the distinctions between the role of supervisor and mentor exist and must be acknowledged, both of these men engaged in long-term relationships with me focused on my leadership development and personal growth. Mentoring relationships can co-exist with other defined relationships if we are clear about role definition and expectations. Mentors encourage mentorees to realize their potential. Leaders encourage followers to make their best contribution to the shared mission of the organization. Mentors have a broader focus on character and leadership; leaders a narrower organizational focus on mission and community. But both relationships exist primarily for the development of the mentoree/follower. And both relationships contribute to the growth and learning of the mentor/leader.

Relational leadership, I believe, embraces the promise of mentoring.

Managers can be mentors. And so can employees. Two significant mentors in my leadership development were employees for whose success I was responsible. When I accepted appointment as President of Regent College, I moved to Canada and assumed responsibilities beyond my experience. I knew I needed help. Max De Pree continued to be a wise mentor with whom I could safely sort out my priorities, but we identified two areas (at least) where my experience and knowledge lagged behind my responsibilities. The first was Canada. Like many in the United States, I thought of Canada as a familiar extension to the North – more like another state than a different culture. Wrong! Canadians may speak the same language, but they have their own history, traditions, and culture with subtle differences that can trip up a new president. If I was going to travel across this country, recruiting students, raising money, and representing the school, I had a steep learning curve about things Canadian. Doug Bennett became my mentor. Doug was Vice President for Development, several years older than me, and had considerable experience in corporate and educational leadership across Canada. Early on we defined a mentoring relationship that existed alongside of our organizational relationship. Doug taught me what I needed to know, raised questions to help me understand what I was learning, corrected my cultural faux pas, and pointed me toward resources to enrich my perspective. The mentoring side of our relationship began with my need for an orientation to Canada. But it continued for nearly ten years as I found in Doug Bennett a wise and trusted counselor with whom to test my thinking about leadership and my visions for the institution. A good mentor has the courage to tell us what we need to know and ask the questions we might avoid.

Finance was the other area where my learning curve was steepest. I could barely read a balance sheet, and Greek was clearer to me than an audited financial statement. So I sought out Art Mooney. Art was the Controller at the college – a gentle man with a solid grasp of financial realities. Organizationally, he reported to me; I was responsible for his success. But when it came to financial management, it was obvious who was the veteran. I took Art to lunch and asked him to be my mentor, to teach me the questions that I needed to ask to safeguard the financial integrity of the school, to guide my learning, and to provide a place where I could think through my financial decisions. For three years Art served as mentor in this area of my life and nurtured an important part of my leadership development.

The question arises here about potential conflict between organizational roles and the mentoring relationship. I have not found that to be a problem. A relational approach to leadership overlaps significantly with mentoring relationships. They share the same basic DNA. In all relationships there are two unique individuals involved, each with their own role and responsibilities. A good relationship – leadership, mentoring, parenting, or friendship – does not ask either participant to abdicate their role or responsibilities. Asking a person to be a mentor requires a certain humility and vulnerability, but so does leadership. The critical variable is communication – open and honest communication. While relational leadership makes little use of authority, there were times when I needed to make the decision and decide against a recommendation of Doug Bennett or Art Mooney. That was why the board appointed me. And I can remember clearly being called into Glenn Barker's office as a young administrator and told bluntly to change a particular behavior. I disagreed and was probably angry at the moment. But I did what was required and it gave us something to talk about in mentoring sessions to follow. A good leadership relationship transcends disagreements and a good mentoring relationship builds on them.

An exercise in reflection

Mentors have played a critical role throughout my life. As I have walked this journey of leadership, I found myself often on unfamiliar paths. Along the way I have continued to seek out mentors who, like the Sherpas in Nepal, can guide me along a portion of the trail. Leadership, like life, is about the journey. There is no destination. We have never arrived. On the trek to the Mount Everest Base Camp we would ask the Sherpas what the trail was like tomorrow. They would laugh and respond: "It's like every Himalayan trail: up and down, up and down." Sherpas and mentors are there to guide us up steep learning curves and through frustrating downturns. As long as I keep walking, I believe I will need mentors to point the way and encourage my progress.

Some relationships are for the long term; Max and I have been working together for over twenty-two years. Some are short term, defined by a specific objective, coincidence of paths, changes in priorities, or even death. At the end of Chapter 3, I encouraged you to reflect on the men and women who joined your path and walked a portion with you. While reading this chapter I hope your mind again wandered, both soaring back over those who have shaped who you have become and hovering for a while over the men and women to whom you now look for guidance and growth.

Before reading further, I would encourage you to stop for another time of reflection. Review your timeline and focus on the present. Who are your mentors now? Whom do you seek out intentionally to work with you on your continued growth and development? Would they consider themselves your mentors? How do you keep yourself renewed? How do you keep learning? What are you doing about your own continued leadership development? How are your current mentors helping you become the person you intend to be? We need to keep learning and there are rich resources around us who could serve as mentors and guides on our journey. The choice is ours.

5. Relationship

Mentoring lies at the heart of relational leadership

What is mentoring?

What have I learned about mentoring from these men and women who joined my leadership journey? There are several things I would identify from these experiences and the reading I have done. I am sure you can add to this list as you reflect on the people who walk your path with you.

Earlier I defined mentoring as *an intentional, exclusive, intensive, voluntary relationship between two persons* – a teaching/learning connection between two persons in which both persons work to nurture the relationship and contribute to the connection. Traditionally we tend to think of mentors as wise experienced gurus taking in hand the young inexperienced protégé and directing his or her development. There is an element of this in mentoring, but I believe there is much more mutuality in the relationship and much more responsibility for learning in the hands of the mentoree.

Gordon Shea, in a fine little workbook, defines mentoring as "a developmental caring, sharing and helping relationship where one person invests time, know-how and effort in enhancing another person's growth, knowledge and skills – responding to critical needs in the life of another person in ways that prepare that person for greater performance, productivity or achievement in the future."[1] He sees a mentor as one who brings knowledge, wisdom, or perspective into a relationship that goes beyond organizationally defined roles. The mentoree then is one who seeks out such help and takes responsibility for his or her own leadership development. Chip Bell softens this a little. He says that "A mentor is simply someone who helps someone else learn something that he or she would have learned less well, more slowly, or not at all if left alone. Notice the power-free nature of this definition! Mentors are not power figures. *Mentors are learning coaches – sensitive, trusted advisors...* We are fellow travelers on this journey toward wisdom."[2]

As we move through this chapter, I would like to loosen the definition further. Mentoring is intentional, exclusive, intensive, and voluntary. It is a teaching and learning relationship between two persons. It is *intentional* if the mentoree recognizes a need for learning and seeks out a resource mentor. But is unilateral intention sufficient? I have been deeply impacted by reading and spending time with management consultant Peter Block. He has been a powerful influence in my life. But the relationship is one-sided. Peter's participation has not been intentional. We did meet once, and he seemed to benefit from the encounter as I did. But he has not committed himself to a mentoring relationship. I continue to read his works and allow his ideas to nurture my thinking. Is Peter Block a mentor for my leadership development? With a looser definition of mentoring, some would say yes. But this experience is not as powerful as the relationship I have with Max De

Pree, where both of us are committed to the mentoring process over the long term. At its heart, mentoring is a relationship with intentional involvement by both persons.

Mentoring is *exclusive* in the sense that it is focused on the growth of a particular mentoree *as perceived by that mentoree*. Mentoring is shaped by mentorees who accept responsibility for their own development. In my formal definition this would normally mean two persons in a relationship of learning and teaching. But the exclusive element is the perception of the mentoree. I am not intentionally mentoring when I speak to a large audience, even if I meet with them often over a period of time. However, someone in the audience may be attracted to my ideas, read my writings, and even contact me with questions. The mentoree determines if this is a mentoring relationship – not the mentor. The initiative and the definition rest with the mentoree, but the mentor also needs to make some level of commitment to the mentoree. It takes two persons to make a relationship.

Mentoring is *intensive* in that it normally has focus. The learning needs of the mentorees define where mentoring is desired, and the mentoring relationships intentionally focus on the mentorees developing vision, values, perspective, knowledge, or skills.

Mentoring is *voluntary*, and in this capacity differs from parenting, teaching, or managing. Mentorees choose mentors to guide them along a particular portion of their journey. It is always about choice. Both mentor and mentoree choose to commit themselves to this learning relationship. Academic institutions and many organizations do assign mentors as coaches or advisors. But even here it will only be a successful mentoring relationship if both parties choose to engage and participate.

And mentoring is always a relationship between two persons. Elsewhere I define leadership as a relationship of influence in which one person seeks to influence the vision, values, attitudes, or behaviors of another.[3] It is always a relationship, and leadership only occurs when the follower perceives the influence and chooses to respond. Mentoring works the same way. Leaders may seek to influence an organization or group of people but leadership occurs only when an individual chooses to accept that influence. It is exactly the same with mentoring. Mentoring happens when one person chooses to listen to and learn from another. Below I will suggest that mentoring can occur in a group setting, but it still is primarily about one person choosing to learn from another. At its heart mentoring is about relationship.

Mentoring is a relationship

It is a relationship that, like all relationships, must be cultivated and nurtured. Like all living things, mentoring relationships will deteriorate if not maintained. It is important to understand the relational nature of mentoring.[4] Like marriage, mentoring is a relationship between two people that takes its shape and definition from the two parties in relationship. There is no formula, no ideal model, and no program of steps to success. It is a relationship – and relationships resist definition. It exists whenever two (or more) persons commit themselves to the connection between them and work to nurture it. Mentoring is a relationship connected by a shared interest in learning and growth and it must be constantly recreated.[5]

The mentoring relationship is more than friendship, more than simply enjoying another's company. Mentoring is focused on learning and growth. Both parties are committed to learning, even though the agenda may be set by the mentoree. Friends can be mentors and mentors are friends. But mentoring has a purpose and a structure defined by the learning needs of the mentoree and shaped by the wisdom and experience of the mentor. The relationship exists for the sake of that purpose – the agenda of the mentoree.

Similarly, mentoring is more than leadership. Good leaders seek to be mentors and create space for people to grow into their potential.[6] But leadership, as noted above, nurtures personal development in the context of organizational objectives. Mentoring, on the other hand, may nurture organizational competence but always in the context of personal development and growth. Mentoring is about mentorees becoming the persons they intend to be. It has both a narrower focus (a person) and a broader focus (life) than organizationally defined leadership.

For that reason mentoring is more about journey than about destination, more about growth than objectives. We travel together on the path of life and leadership, not to reach a final plateau or summit, but to engage the journey fully. Here Laurent Daloz sounds like one of my Sherpa guides.

> How, then, do mentors transmit wisdom? Most often, it seems, they take us on a journey. In this aspect of their work, *mentors are guides.* They lead us along the journey of our lives. We trust them because they have been there before. They embody our hopes, cast light on the way ahead, interpret arcane signs, warn us of lurking dangers, and point out unexpected delights along the way. There is a certain luminosity about them, and they often pose as magicians in tales of transformation, for *magic* is a word given to what we cannot see – and we can rarely see across the gulf.[7]

Mentoring is a teaching and learning relationship between two travelers on the journey. Each brings a unique perspective, a particular experience and a desire to grow in the relationship. And both mentor and mentoree benefit from their time together.

Mentoring in learning communities

At its core, mentoring is an intentional learning relationship between two (or more) persons, where one or both persons share from their life and experiences the wisdom of their heart and mind, and where one or both persons give the other the trust to hold them accountable to their stated vision and values. How often, who initiates, and what agenda are all determined uniquely by the parties involved. I do not think there is one best model or one right model. What is important is trust, honesty, and a relationship of belonging, encouragement, affirmation, accountability, and hope.

Most of the illustrations I have given in this book are one-on-one, individual, face-to-face mentoring relationships. This is the primary model I have in mind, probably because this has been the most powerful and transformational model on my journey. However, there is another form that mentoring relationships can take. I believe that some of the same benefits – encouragement, affirmation, perspective, and challenge – can be found in small groups of persons committed to one another's leadership and growth. Three such groups important in my life emerged during the middle management years of my leadership journey. The first was a group of other middle managers, some within the same organization that I served and some from outside. We met weekly for breakfast with the specific agenda of encouraging one another in our leadership development and holding one another accountable for pursuing our priorities and living our values. That group met for several years until, one by one, we moved off into new leadership responsibilities. After a gap of over thirteen years, however, we had a reunion of that group recently. It was good to remember together the early days of our leadership development and be encouraged by the opportunities and challenges facing each of us in our current leadership roles. In some ways a group is not as intimate as a one-on-one mentoring relationship. In other ways it is easier to hold ourselves accountable when we have the multiple commitments of the group. I do believe there is an important role for peer groups of leaders – what I like to call *"learning communities"* – where leaders belong, where they have something to offer and something to learn, where they feel safe enough to think out loud, and where they find encouragement, affirmation, and hope. The mentored learning is still individual; it is the responsibility of the mentoree. In one sense the group takes on almost a corporate role, relating like an individual to the leader. At the same time, group relationships provide multiple lines of accountability and diversity of perspective as we encourage each other's leadership journey.[8]

My second accountability or mentoring group is not directly related to leadership, but has taught me much about leadership, relationships, community, and life. This is a group of men with whom I climb mountains. Several are in leadership and management roles; several are professional psychologists. We share in common a love of the mountains and we have climbed, hiked, and canoed together now for over twenty-nine years. In the seventies we spent one three-day weekend in the California Sierra's every month for six years, missing only five months in that six years. As our responsibilities began to scatter us around North America, we dropped that to three or four trips per year. Now we try to get together at least twice each year, and gather as much for the friendship and encouragement in our life responsibilities as we do for our love of the mountains. Twenty-nine years of shared life builds very strong bonds and gives intimate insight into each other's lives. It is normal for members of the group to be in conversation by telephone or email – counseling, advising, coaching, and mentoring one another through our various responsibilities. There is much "mentoring" wisdom in this group, and we learn much about life and leadership from each other, as well as in the organization and safe execution of a mountain climbing expedition. And, of course, there is very high trust. "What is said on the trail stays on the trail!" In a way, the group itself corporately becomes the mentor to each of its members, as well as the context that sustains a network of valuable accountability relationships.

The third model of learning community I have experienced flowed directly from an encounter with Harvey Cox, the Harvard theologian. If, as Max De Pree believes, mentors ask the questions that open windows onto our future, then Harvey Cox might qualify as what some call a "passive mentor"[9] of mine. In 1970 my wife Beverly and I attended a lecture by Dr. Cox on the breakdown of family in the United States. He lifted up the human need for intimacy, lamented the disappearance of extended family, church, and community as resources for intimacy, and argued that the marriage relationship alone could not bear the level of intimacy we need to survive in this life. He concluded with questions: With whom are you intimate? Where do you have the depth of relationships to sustain you on your journey? Who will stand with you during the good times and the bad times and help you learn along the way? Beverly and

I walked out of that lecture and chose to change the nature of our journey. We called together several couples, shared what we had heard and formed what was to be the first of a series of small groups to provide intimacy and accountability in our lives. Now, for nearly thirty-four years, Beverly and I have participated in at least one such group meeting weekly. These are mentoring groups – four or five couples committed to meet weekly, to share our life journeys, and hold one another accountable for learning and growth – guiding one another through the ups and downs of marriage, parenting, career and vocation, sickness and health. This is a place where people have permission to ask each other the questions we need to face as we negotiate pathways through life. Every person in the group is working on particular growth areas at each stage of our journey. This too is mentoring.

Mentoring at a distance

Mentoring can take a variety of forms, but at its heart it is still about relationship. And in today's world of tech-nology, relationships are increasingly going "online." Is there a place for *e-mentoring* or *tele-mentoring?* Yes, if there is relationship and mutual commitment to learning and growth. I have not been willing to engage in a mentoring relationship as mentor or as mentoree that was *solely based* on email or telephone. I need to see someone face to face, to listen to body language as well as words. For me, relationships are built over time with face-to-face interaction – shared geography – and must be nurtured and tended with more than words. Established mentoring relationships can be continued by email or telephone but eventually need to be nurtured and replenished with face-to-face reality. I can draw much mentoring wisdom from Sam but only because I see him face-to-face at least twice each year. Several persons with whom I have had face-to-face mentoring relationships are now living in different countries. The mentoring relationships continue, but almost entirely by email or telephone. This is possible because of the extended time we spent together at the beginning. And even now when paths can cross we arrange a lunch or dinner to renew the relationship. Similarly, the mountaineering group is scattered across the United States but we maintain email and telephone mentoring, enriched by our trips together each year.

Up to this point I have declined to serve as mentor to persons who have asked to initiate and conduct the relationship by letter, email, or telephone. It does not fit my concept of relationship. But I may be limited in my thinking here. There are several mentoring programs for teens that use technology exclusively, building on the chat room relationships of today's teenagers.[10] The relationship, however, is the critical component and relationships take time to cultivate and sustain in person and online.

> The key to successful long-distance mentoring is taking time to establish the human connection and develop a relationship. Generally listservs and on-line discussion do not include that opportunity.
>
> Many mentors underestimate the time commitment required to establish and build long-distance mentoring relationships. In general, time is a major factor in establishing, building, and sustaining mentoring relationships. In long-distance mentoring, making the connection is a formidable task and requires time and tending.[11]

Many people find it easier to be honest and vulnerable online than in person, so I am sure that a level of mentoring will be possible as online relationships develop.[12] Like Harvey Cox, I believe that human beings need intimacy, and intimacy for me demands physical presence at some point. Even online relationships will be nurtured by face-to-face interaction as we travel our journeys together.

Defining the relationship

Early in the mentoring relationship, mentor and mentoree need to clarify expectations and define the parameters of the relationship. The roles and responsibilities of each person need to be understood. Some ground rules that seem to emerge in most relationships:

Mentoring focuses on the one being mentored, not the mentor   Again, this focus on the mentoree needs to be underlined as critical to the definition of mentoring. It is about the learning and development of the mentoree. It is not about cloning the mentor. It is not even about passing on the mentor's wisdom and values. That may happen, but the purpose of the mentoring relationship is unique: to create space for the mentoree to engage in the self-learning and self-management that allows the mentoree to become the person he or she intends to be. The mentor is a resource and guide along the way. The agenda is set by the learning needs of the mentoree. Mentors do not shape mentorees. They ask the questions and provide the encouragement for mentorees to shape themselves.

Mentoring includes the vulnerable sharing of one's self   Mentors offer who they are, what they know, what they are learning. They bring their strengths and their weaknesses to the relationship. Mentors are often chosen because they model the kind of person the mentoree wants to become. However, mentors are growing and changing like everyone else. The ability to reflect on and share the process of growth and life is a gift for the mentor as well as for those being mentored. While particular experiences and skills can be beneficial to those being mentored, the core exchange of the mentoring process is a sharing of persons – a sharing of one's heart and mind, one's values and commitments. It is the person of the mentor that leaves the lasting legacy, not the positions held or the experiences accumulated.

At its heart, mentoring is a relationship, a caring connection between two persons. As such, it is rich with possibilities for learning but also filled with risk. Mentoring is a sharing of one's self, letting someone into the mentor's life and experience, sharing the mentor's successes and failures. In such relationships who we really are, what we really believe becomes evident. When mentors and mentorees open their hearts and minds to one another they make themselves vulnerable – that is the heartbeat of mentoring. Trust and confidentiality of course are essential for this level of vulnerability. Mentors share of themselves so that mentorees can become who they intend to be. Mentors do not ask mentorees to be like them, only to learn from their experience as they make their own choices in life. Mentoring allows mentorees access to the mentor's life to encourage mentorees along their own journey, and it invites the mentor into the life of the mentoree as guide and companion.

Mentoring includes forgiveness Mentors are human beings with flaws and failings. We like to think of mentors as those who are above us, beyond us, on a pedestal, models of success. And they may well be. But they are always human beings – flawed, wounded – seeking to understand, live, and contribute to life.[13] Mentors may let you down. You may let your mentors down. Any strong relationship must carry within it the commitment to forgive and give trust again if the relationship is to survive for the long haul. The same is true for the mentoring relationship. Only forgiveness and commitment can sustain a relationship over time and that is precisely when we learn the most about our leadership and ourselves.

Mentoring is more about following than leading   When we choose a mentor from whom to learn, we choose to follow a person, to allow that person – that mentor – to influence our thinking, our vision, our values, our behavior. That is leadership. Mentors do exercise leadership – but they do so at the invitation of the follower. Mentoring is more about followership than leadership. This is important, because the persons we choose to follow become the persons who shape who we become – the character that forms our leadership. Leaders begin as followers. This is true for all of life. We begin life by following parents, teachers, and coaches. Who we follow contributes to who we become. For leaders, the importance of mentoring lies in the reality that who we choose to follow shapes our leadership. Leadership emerges out of followership.

Mentoring is mutually beneficial   Relationships are reciprocal. The mentoring relationship is not an exception. We choose mentors to follow and learn from as we walk our journey and form our leadership. But mentorees are not the only ones to profit from this learning exchange. Mentors benefit from the mentoring relationship as well as the one seeking a mentor. If the mutual benefit is not there, the relationship will not last. Both parties bring something to contribute. Both parties must believe that they are receiving value from their investment.

Mentoring requires an appropriate fit There must be sufficient common ground upon which to build a mentoring relationship – probably a common pool of shared values is a pre-requisite. Shared experience, shared vision, and compatible personalities all will play a role. Not every pairing of persons will produce a lasting mentoring relationship. A comfortable fit – the ability to enjoy and appreciate one another's company – is necessary for any long-term relationship.

Mentoring involves listening and asking questions Mentors listen well and carefully. They also ask questions. Max De Pree believes this is one of the most important things any leader can learn: to ask good questions. Mentors are not the place to go for answers. Good mentoring listens and questions. The learning is the responsibility of the one being mentored. It is so easy for us to ask a mentor what to do. It is also too easy for many of us to answer and tell someone what to do. But good mentoring resists this. Mentoring is about listening and questioning, not about answering or giving direction.

Mentoring sustains relational leadership Leadership is a relationship of influence. As Max De Pree says, it is a serious meddling in other people's lives. Leadership is a precarious responsibility. For the sake of the people who look to them for leadership, leaders need wisdom. They need perspective. They need accountability. This is the role that mentoring plays.

At one point during my tenure as president I came to the conclusion that I was failing as a leader. I did not believe my leadership was having the influence needed at that time in the college's development. I decided I should probably admit I was not up to the challenge and resign. However, because of my great respect for Max De

Pree, I did not think I should resign until I had talked with him. I probably wanted his blessing even in my failure, perhaps especially in my failure. So I flew back to Grand Rapids for a day of mentoring. I shared my thoughts and found myself weeping as I acknowledged my struggle and asked for his wisdom. It is hard to admit failure, especially to someone you respect so highly. And of course he listened and gave me his full blessing and encouragement, whether I resigned or stayed on. And of course I didn't resign. I needed a safe place to think through what was not working and why. And in the context of that conversation I recommitted to the vision that brought me into the position. I stayed another six years.

Every leader needs one or more mentors to provide the depth of reflection necessary to sustain vision and energy for leadership. I also believe every leader needs to serve as a mentor – because the mentor learns as much from the process as the one being mentored. Teachers have long known that the teacher learns more than the student. This may well be true for mentors also. The relationship of mentoring causes intentional reflection and keeps the mentor thinking about life, leadership, vision, and values and holds up a mirror to keep us accountable to the priorities to which we are committed. Everyone needs a mentor. And everyone needs to be a mentor.

What makes a good mentor?

The effectiveness of a mentor will always be determined by the perception of the mentoree. We seek out persons who can help us sort out our choices and define our leadership as we journey through life. There is not an ultimate or ideal template for being an effective mentor. Each mentoree will bring his or her own list of characteristics important to the learning relationship. Here are some important questions in assessing potential as a mentor – questions to ponder as you reflect on the mentoring relationship.

- *Why do you respect this person and the life, leadership, and wisdom he models?*
- *How accurate is her understanding of her own journey?*
- *Who have been his mentors?*
- *How articulately does she reflect on her life, experience, and learning?*
- *What is his philosophy or theology of management?*
- *What has she learned lately – is she still learning and growing?*
- *What does openness, transparency, and honest speaking mean to him?*
- *When does he listen and when does he talk?*
- *How is her strength of character revealed in her values and integrity?*
- *How does he handle conflict and diversity?*
- *What does she encourage and affirm?*
- *Why does she believe in your potential?*
- *How well does she understand your agenda for development?*
- *What will being accessible mean to him?*
- *What gives her hope?*

6. Growth

Mentoring reflects on the hope of relational leadership

He walked into my office, tall, handsome and confident. He came to talk about mentoring. We chatted for a while about his work and journey and finally he said, "I need a mentor." As a confirmed believer in the value of mentoring, I commended his interest and asked why. His answer disappointed me, but also began to tell me something about him: "Some of the people who work with me think I need a mentor and they suggested that you would be a good person to talk with." So I pushed a little further: "Do you think you need a mentor?" "Yes," he responded, "A mentor would look good on my resume." Discouragement displaced my disappointment. So we talked. He wanted to advance in leadership responsibilities, but was regularly passed over when openings occurred. He thought having a mentor on his resume would help. When I asked if there were areas of learning or development that he wanted to explore he could think of nothing. Simply getting a recognized name as a mentor on his resume would be enough. And then, of course, the next question: "So, could you be my mentor?" Not a propitious beginning for a mentoring relationship. I asked him, "Why me?" He responded that others had told him I was a good mentor. I asked him what he knew about me. He responded, "Nothing." He had not read anything I had written, had never heard me speak, and this was the first time he had even seen me. When I asked how he thought I might help, he came back to the resume, "Having the director of the De Pree Center as a mentor on my resume would help." For obvious reasons I did not agree to be his mentor. However, I did not turn him down completely. I gave him a copy of my book on relational leadership and suggested that he read the book and if he still thought I could be of assistance to come back with some specific ideas about what he would like to work on. That was seven months ago. I have not heard from him again. Mentors are not names on a resume. They are resources to assist persons in their own self-directed leadership development.

Mentoring at its heart is self-directed leadership development that takes seriously the relational nature of leadership. It is always about the mentoree, about the choices of the mentoree, about the growth of the mentoree. While mentors play critical roles in this process, mentoring is always about the mentoree. This is where it starts. Mentoring for leadership begins with a personal self-assessment that there is a need for learning, an area where growth is desired. And because leadership is a relationship, mentors become partners who en-courage us along this learning journey. Mentors influence and affirm. But mentorees choose whether they will learn, grow, and become the leaders they are capable of being. Mentoring is a leadership relationship in which both mentor and mentoree add value and benefit, but at its core, mentoring is a relationship of learning directed by the mentoree.

So, while I believe there is a place for the Donald Bubnas of this world to walk into someone's life uninvited and encourage their leadership journey, I am increasingly convinced, especially for persons seeking to develop leadership capacity, that the mentoring cycle begins with the mentoree. I said earlier that I did not believe in seven definitive steps to mentoring. So here are twenty steps to get started! This is not a checklist but a description of the process as I have experienced it. Every mentoring relationship will take its character and format from the unique situations and perspectives that the mentor and mentoree bring to the process. I offer here some guidelines to encourage your reflection, beginning with personal assessment.

1. Identify areas open to growth

This is where it begins. Are you open to growth, to learning, to change? A mentoring relationship assumes a shared journey during which two people agree to keep learning and growing. Where are your rough edges? Where are your flat sides? What gaps need to be filled in? What new areas need exploration? In Chapter 8, I identify some of the tensions inherent in the responsibility of leadership. Each of these critical arenas brings a level of ambiguity and uncertainty to the role of the leader. For most of us these are areas in which we continue to learn and to grow. Mentors who have lived with these tensions can help us organize our thinking and lean into the tensions. Each one is a potential area for growth. Similarly, developmental psychologists have identified natural stages through which men and women pass as they move from young adulthood through midlife into maturity.[1] And organizational psychologists have identified the developmental cycles of organizations with concomitant expectations for leadership.[2] Each of these transition points, each fork in the trail, each summit, plateau, or valley on the journey of life and leadership reveals potential areas for growth. Effective leaders continually learn and identify areas in which they need to grow.

2. Identify someone from whom you can learn

Mentor resources are all around us. A person does not have to be perfect – few people are, but he or she should be strong in the area in which you want to grow. Your mentor does not need to be older, nor does he or she need to be seasoned in all areas of life. Often someone younger has knowledge of subjects like technology, cultural understanding, or finance where you are lacking. Do you respect the person and the strength that person brings to you? On what basis do you assess the contribution this person could make to your growth and learning? Be sure you have done your homework and have accurately assessed the strengths the person brings and the possible match with your learning needs. The "resume" concept of mentoring with which I began this chapter is a distortion. Potential mentors do not need to be great leaders, recognized stars; but they do need to be great persons whom you respect and with whom you believe you can address your identified areas for growth.

3. Ask for one meeting (lunch?); interview your prospective mentor and listen to his or her thoughts on your subject

You don't have to announce your interest in a mentoring relationship at the beginning. It might be asking too much for a yet untested relationship. Asking someone to be your mentor before building the relationship is like asking for marriage before the first date. Many persons with wisdom to share find it intimidating to think of themselves as mentors. For some this is humility. For others it is a misunderstanding of the role of the mentor.

Take it one meeting at a time while you test the relationship. Ask for a conversation about a particular topic with a perspective mentor. Ask for only one meeting. Suggest you would like to ask some questions, hear their wisdom, and gain insights from your prospect's experience. If you can, eat a meal together for this first meeting, and pay attention to the social side of the time together. You may have noticed from my stories that I spend a lot of time over meals: the donut shop, Ernie Jr.'s Taco House, the restaurant with Max De Pree. Nearly all of my mentoring relationships – as mentor and as mentoree – happen around food. This is not accidental. There is something about a shared meal that nurtures the relational side of mentoring. It is neither a classroom nor a counseling session. It is a social relationship of mutual learning and shared respect. A meal enhances the relationship and levels the roles a little. Ask them to lunch. And pay for their lunch! When I ask for a mentoring meeting, I always expect to pay for the meal. And when someone asks me to such a meeting, I assume that they will be paying. In fact, when I am first asked about a mentoring relationship, I usually respond, "Buy me lunch and let's talk about it."

4. Use the first meeting to test for a natural and comfortable relationship

Mentoring is all about a relationship. A continuing relationship depends on both you and your mentor finding the time enjoyable and instructive. Do you share interests? Purposes? Are your values compatible? Recognizing the value of different perspectives, do you simply enjoy having lunch with this person? Do you respect this person? Do you feel respected and encouraged? Could this become a relationship that you could nurture and maintain? This first meeting is a good opportunity to share the timelines of your personal journeys to look for overlaps and gaps. I do not propose pulling out the timelines you developed earlier in this book, but there is benefit in asking questions that allow the prospective mentor (and you) to sketch out your leadership journeys in broad strokes. You can delve more deeply as the relationship matures.

5. Ask for a second meeting or propose a short-term, periodic relationship

If you both find the first meeting comfortable and interesting ask for a second. Schedule just one meeting at a time until the mutual comfort level is strong enough to warrant a commitment to periodic get-togethers. Agree on when, where, and how often you can ask for such meetings. Glenn Barker and I met weekly, often over lunch. Max De Pree and I agreed that I could ask for three to four days of his time over the year, each meeting usually lasting three to four hours over lunch.

6. Take responsibility to arrange the next meeting(s)

Make the next meeting convenient for the mentor and don't expect the mentor to take the initiative. You have more to gain than your mentor does. Your mentor may take the lead later in the relationship, but at the early stages you must provide the momentum, direction and follow through. Remember this is self-directed leadership development. The mentoree takes the initiative and manages the learning process.

7. Take responsibility for the agenda

Come to the meetings with an agenda of things you would like to talk about. Do not assume that your mentor will bring one, even though he or she might. Accept responsibility for using your time together well. When I meet with Max De Pree I always bring an agenda, sometimes a typed out list that I share with him, often a list of topics or questions I have written out for myself. The conversation usually includes some summary of what has happened in our lives and leadership since we last met before it focuses on the particular issues at hand.

8. Come to the meeting with questions

Your agenda should be heavily weighted with questions designed to draw wisdom from your mentor. In addition to questions specific to the area of shared interest, it can be valuable to ask mentors what they have learned lately or what they are reading. Come more as a listener than a talker. The final chapter of this book focuses on the power of questions. It is with questions that we frame the future and open ourselves to learning. Since mentoring reflects on character, values, relationships, and choices, the questions we bring seldom lead to a single answer. Instead they launch conversations that allow both mentor and mentoree to expand their understanding and learn.

9. Invite the person to ask questions that draw you out

From the beginning invite your mentor to ask you questions. Give your permission to discuss anything and everything about you and what you believe. Give permission even to probe behind your words to a truth you might be avoiding or unaware of. Make yourself vulnerable to learning and growth. The questions your mentor asks may be more valuable than answers or advice. Max De Pree is a master at questions; I am still learning. (One of the liabilities of an educator is that we are trained to have answers. Yet we know that the great teachers leave us with questions.) I often say with some humor and much truth that Max De Pree usually answers my questions with a question: "That's a very good question; where does it lead us?" Good questions lead us to think.

10. Listen, assess, act, and give feedback

Listen more than talk. Assess and evaluate what you hear. Sort out the wisdom from the biases or blind spot while watching out for your own biases and blind spots. Remember, mentors are human also. They too are on a journey; they are still learning. Act on the wisdom. Mentors will not stay long with people who fail to act on what they learn. Talk without action is a waste of time. Act and report at the next meeting on what you learned, what you tried, what worked and what did not, and be prepared with questions to explore the matter more fully. It was not until after several meetings that I realized Max kept notes on our conversations. He kept track of our discussions and watched to see what I was learning and what I was doing. Mentors make an investment in your development. They want to see the return on their investment. The opportunity to interact with you and watch the conversation worked out in your leadership is also a way mentors keep learning.

11. Ask for another meeting

Don't forget that the momentum for your relationship is up to you. Ask for, schedule and follow through with the next meeting. The mentoring relationship will continue only as long as you continue to initiate the meetings and learn from your conversations. The burden to remember what has been discussed also falls primarily on you not on the mentor. This is true even though a good mentor who respects your leadership will keep track of your progress. One further note here: as Max De Pree says in the foreword, the meetings should be planned with the convenience of the mentor in mind. I always go to my mentor, and I expect mentorees to come to me whether I am at home or on the road. Mentors give of their time and wisdom. Mentorees are responsible to make meetings happen.

12. It is not important to call your conversations a "mentoring relationship"

This learning relationship between two people may well become a formal mentoring partnership – intentional, exclusive, intensive and voluntary. But such acknowledgment is not important and may, in fact, put too much weight, too many expectations on the relationship in the early stages. It is much more important that two people find their time together a fruitful investing in and learning from one another. Along the way – or even in hindsight – you might begin to call it a mentoring relationship.

Mentoring has long been a powerful strategy for leadership development. It is the natural approach for personal renewal and development when leadership is recognized as relationship rather than position or person. This book is a witness to the gift of mentors in life and leadership. However, like many terms in the vocabulary of leadership and management, "mentor" has been used so broadly that it ranges from teacher or model to hero or guru or saint. It carries too much baggage. So even though I champion the concept of this powerful learning relationship and want to clarify its definition, I find it best to use the word "mentor" as little as possible. The label might be appropriate when your relationship is strong enough not to need a label at all.

Mentoring is self-directed leadership development – a teaching and learning relationship. It begins with the mentoree. It starts with the mentoree's need for growth. But if that is where it stops, we probably did not learn enough. Mentoring leads you to see the potential in other people and to open yourself to helping them see that potential, which leads to the next step.

13. Identify someone with potential whose values you respect

Once you have experienced the advantages of a mentor, look around for people with potential whom you can encourage. Look for someone you respect, whose values you can affirm, someone who you believe has potential to grow. If the mentoring relationship is valuable for leadership development, it will produce leaders with a high commitment to growing other leaders. This is what leadership is all about – creating space for people to realize their potential and make their best contribution to the shared mission – to become leaders themselves, with competence and confidence to influence others. Leaders who have been mentored look for persons with potential.

14. Find opportunities to affirm lavishly this person's contribution

Look for chances to approach and affirm this person and his or her work. Be lavish in honest affirmation. Do not offer to be a mentor unless you have been asked, perhaps even if you are asked. Affirm generously and wait to see if anything develops. Given the tensions of leadership and the ambiguities of the journey, most people need affirmation and encouragement to move forward with hope. Recognition, gratitude, and praise acknowledge potential and lift the spirit.

15. Find opportunities to encourage personally

Look for chances to encourage the other person by sharing of yourself, your resources, your connections, and your relationships. Be a person whose very presence is encouraging and empowering. Again, do not offer to be a mentor or even offer to help unless you are asked. Be open to possibilities. If the other person wants to take things further, be available. Encouragement and affirmation are powerful forces. However, the attention of a respected leader can be both gratifying and terrifying. Let the other person decide if and when they see this becoming a more focused relationship.

16. Listen to words, emotions and body language

In the mentoring relationship, listen. Listen to the words spoken, but listen even more carefully to the words not spoken. Listen to the emotions, the feelings, the joy, the hurt, the anger, the love being communicated. Try to hear what is going on inside the person's heart as well as head. You have the privilege of hearing things that the other person may not even know he or she is saying. It is the emotional, affective side of relationships that suggest some face-to-face interaction. You need to be able to listen behind the spoken word and read between the lines of written word. Listening may be the most important skill you bring to the relationship.

17. Ask questions rather than give advice

Think questions, questions, and more questions. When people ask for advice, resist the advice that leaps into your mind. Form a question instead that draws wisdom and learning from the other person. Try to help the person to see another view of reality through the questions you ask rather than through lessons you expound upon. Questions are relational; they create choice. Advice narrows perspective and may limit possibilities. The quality of the relationship will be found in the questions you ask.

18. Consider what you can learn from that person

All relationships are mutual. It takes two persons to sustain a relationship. A mentoring relationship is no different. Both people must see their time together as a learning, growing experience. What can you learn by sharing the learning and growth of the other person? What can you learn from the reality in which the person lives and works? What can you learn from the unique person and perspective of the other?

19. Identify areas open to growth

This brings us back to the beginning. Are you still open to growth, to learning, to change? A mentoring relationship assumes a shared journey with two people who know they must keep learning and growing. Where are your rough edges these days? Where are your flat sides? What gaps need to be filled in at this stage of your journey through the reality in which you find yourself? What can you begin to explore as you continue to discover the world around you?

20. Identify someone from whom you can learn

From whom are you learning? Who are your mentors now? Who believes you have potential? Whom do you respect? Whose conversations and questions will enrich your life? Good mentors continue to learn. In most cases they have mentors themselves. And the cycle continues.

The mentoring process is a cycle. Someone comes alongside, sees potential and gives us encouragement.

We seek them out to learn from their experience. We take the initiative. We manage the relationship. We direct the learning. And we make the choices that form our character and shape our leadership. As we grow and develop in our leadership capacity we see people with potential. Because we have had mentors, we know the value and we know what to do. So we come alongside and give encouragement. The rest is up to the person we encourage. And the cycle continues and leadership is developed.

The young man who wanted a mentor for his resume never returned. Perhaps he found his mentor elsewhere – perhaps not. The initiative is his. And so different from Rory. Rory contacted me with a very specific agenda. He was already in senior leadership, but he was an engineer more comfortable with structures than relationships. He wanted to talk about leadership and community. How do we nurture relationships and build community in an organization with accountability and productivity? Now that is an agenda that energizes me! But Rory is another story.

7. Promise

Memorising reflects on the potential of relational leadership

The letter was from South Africa. I recognized the name. Dr Rory Prest was the General Secretary of SCO, a national university student organization headquartered in Cape Town. I had met Rory ten years earlier when he was doing graduate study in Canada. Since that time I had followed his successful leadership at SCO from a distance. I saw his potential and his passion. He was a very bright young man – a PhD in engineering – more comfortable with structures than with the relationships of community. But he was a man deeply committed to racial reconciliation and community building in his organization. He wrote to ask if I would mentor him through a nine-month study leave, helping him think about building community and reconciliation into the national organization he led. I shared some of his passions and knew I would learn from his perspectives. Wanting to encourage him in his vision and his leadership, I agreed. Rory brought his family to Canada for a year of stimulating conversations about life, leadership, relationships, and community. We met for several hours every other week during that year; he would read and reflect and come eager to test his thinking and engage with my questions. That was a busy year. In fact I had just resigned from my position as President of Regent College and was heavily committed to a healthy, celebrative leadership transition for our community. So I had to make an intentional choice to invest that much time in Rory.

What Do Mentors Look For?

What do mentors look for in a person in whom they will invest themselves? We have limited time and limited abilities. What makes a person an attractive candidate for mentoring? Some characteristics suggest themselves to me. They are as follows:

Potential   Does the person have possibilities for learning and growth? Can you see talent, giftedness, abilities that just need some encouragement to develop? At one level, I believe that everyone has unrealized potential to grow and thus is a candidate for mentoring. Many persons have seeds of talent or character that still reside below the surface and just need a little sunlight and water. Timely encouragement can release creativity and new life. The key is whether you see it or not. If the mentor sees the untapped potential, it opens new possibilities for growth. If you don't see the possibilities, it does not necessarily mean the person has no potential; it only means that you are probably not a good mentor for that person. Can you see potential that you want to nurture?

Curiosity and a desire to learn   Is the person continuing to learn? Is she still making connections and seeking understanding? Does he look for new fields to study or disciplines to explore? Is growth a priority? Someone who thinks he has nothing to learn is a risky investment. This of course is one of the dangers of leadership. Persons in visible roles of leadership are not always willing to acknowledge the vulnerability of still needing to grow. With the inherent ambiguities of leadership, a person without curiosity and a desire to learn is a liability to the organization.

Strength of character   Does this person know who he is, what he believes, what he stands for? Is there integrity between words and actions? Does she know herself well enough to be comfortable with new ideas, with conflict, with diversity of opinion? Can the person reflect on the experiences of life and relish the continued formation of character?

Shared values   I do not believe it is necessary for mentor and mentoree to work from a shared value framework. There is much to learn from people who can articulate the application of their values, even when they differ. However, so much of the mentoring relationship is about character development that shared values will facilitate the process. Unless the purpose of the mentoring is focused on value clarification, the relationship probably will work more smoothly if both parties are operating with compatible values systems. If the values differ greatly, the relationship may not thrive.

Reflective thinking and self assessment   Hand in hand with character and values comes self-assessment. How accurate is the person's self-perception? Is he aware of how others see him? Can she transcend the moment and reflect on how she is reacting and why? Accurate self-awareness and self-control are critical. It is very difficult to move someone forward who does not know where he is. Reflective thinking can be nurtured if character is strong and self-assessment is accurate.

Responsibility for one's own growth   This is closely tied to self-assessment. Is the person self-directed? Will she accept responsibility for her own growth or does she see everyone else as the problem? Internally motivated persons make good mentorees. Externally focused persons can move towards entitlement or victimization, and expect the mentor to tell them what to do. This is not mentoring. Mentoring at its heart is about assisted self-directed learning. The initiative rests in the hands of the mentoree. The mentoree is responsible for his or her own development.

Energy   This one is a little harder to describe, and perhaps it is only a personal attraction of mine. I like to work with people of energy, people in whose presence I am refreshed and stimulated. When the person walks into the room do they bring energy? Or do they take energy? That is actually a good question to ask about ourselves, because I think energy is also necessary for a mentor. Do you add energy when you arrive or do you drain the energy of those around you? Relationships require energy.

Purpose   This one also is closely connected to character. Character asks who the person is. Purpose asks why they choose to be who they are – what they are about. Mentors walk with people on their journey; there is purpose. The specific mentoring relationship may focus on a unique purpose, a learning objective, or skill development. But mentors like to see more than that. Who does she intend to be? What contribution does he want to make? What kind of legacy will this person leave behind?

Hope   Mentors want to invest themselves in persons with hope, men and women who believe in the future and want to make it a better place. Hope feeds growth. Hope embraces learning. Hope is curious. Hope replicates itself.

These are some of the things that mentors look for when they choose to invest their lives in a mentoree. It is also the same set of questions I would ask when interviewing a person for employment. Whether mentoree or employee, this is the kind of person that I want to walk alongside and learn with.

Why we mentor others

Mentoring requires something from the mentor. It requires time, commitment and vulnerability to nurture a mentoring relationship. So why do people do it? For many it is a natural response of gratitude for the mentors who have walked with them. Eight of us who have looked to Max De Pree as mentor have agreed that we will gather each year to offer a workshop on mentoring for others because of the debt we believe we owe to Max for his investment in us. And all of us serve actively as mentors. If you have experienced mentors you know what you have to offer. For some, mentoring is an effective way to address the question of legacy. We want to contribute something with our lives that lasts. As we get older it becomes clear that positions, titles, accomplishments, and acquisitions have little to do with legacy. The legacy of a life is found in the relationships around it. It is in relationship that we pass on the hope that has been handed to us. And hope is the promise of mentoring. We mentor because we believe in the future, because we can still see possibilities for making this a better place to live, because we can envision what a person can become, because there is promise.

But there is another reason why we mentor. Mentoring fuels personal growth and renewal in the mentor.[1] The opportunity to reflect critically on our own life and leadership teaches us new truths about ourselves. It is a valuable exercise to articulate what you believe and why, to discuss the connections between your values and your behavior, to review your leadership through a reflective lens. Mentors grow through the vulnerability of self-disclosure and acknowledged learning. Responding to the questions of a mentoree is as formative for the mentor as it is when the mentor asks the questions. This questioning relationship is renewing. There is also the reality of continued learning that comes through the window of the mentoree's experience. As we enter the world of the mentoree – inquiring, exploring, encouraging – we are introduced to another context, a new arena in which to think about our values and reflect on our leadership. The choice to become a mentor is a decision to grow.

Becoming a mentor

The promise of mentoring requires that mentors give thought to why they choose to invest in another. We need to understand our motivations. Why do we do it? Which of the needs listed above is driving our decision? The motivation that brings us to the relationship will have a direct impact on the relationship.[2] And there are less winsome motivations that must be considered. Do we mentor because we seek control? Do we mentor because we need to be perceived as wise? Do we want to be needed? All of us come to our leadership responsibilities with mixed motivations. The effective mentor will spend some time reflecting on those motivations before engaging the mentoree.

Mentors, like mentorees, must understand themselves. The work of Daniel Goleman and others on emotional intelligence suggests that effective leadership and mentoring is grounded on certain emotional competencies.[3] Effective leaders and mentors rate high in self-awareness, self control, social awareness, and relationship management. They have an accurate self-assessment and corresponding confidence. They manage their emotions with transparency, adaptability, learning, initiative, and optimism. They have empathy for the feelings of others and the relational dynamics of community. And they are very good at building relationships. Leadership is a relationship. Mentoring is relationship. The health of the relationship will always be tied to the health of the persons.[4]

Mentors must understand what they will offer and what they cannot offer. It is important up front to recognize your limits, set your boundaries, and clarify expectations. Who are you prepared to be in this relationship? This will change as mentors keep growing. What are you learning these days? As we noted above, there is a connection between learning, hope, and the promise of the future.

Mentors also need to understand what mentoring is and what it is not. Both mentor and mentoree need to understand the terms and agree at the beginning of the relationship. Mentoring is a working relationship focused on learning and growth. It is about active listening and powerful questions. It is therapeutic but it is not therapy. It is empowering but it is not management. Mentoring is an intentional relationship focused primarily on the self-directed growth of the mentoree. It encompasses character and nurtures leadership. It develops skills and nurtures reflection. When crises occur in life or leadership, both mentor and mentoree need to understand the limits of the relationship and assess when professional assistance is needed. To paraphrase Max De Pree, mentoring, like leadership, is a serious meddling in a person's life. We owe it to the person we are mentoring to understand what we are doing and why.

Mentoring models

When we choose to become mentors, the relationships that form will flow from who we are, from the mentors we have experienced, and the life situation in which we find ourselves. Each relationship is unique. The only constant is relationship. Mentoring is always a relationship between two persons (even within a group setting) focused on learning and growth. As I read and observe these relationships they tend to fall into five approximate models: gardener, advisor, manager, coach, or resource.

Gardener   When a gardener walks into the yard, his senses quickly move past the beauty of the roses, the vigor of the salvias, or the fragrance of the basil. He sees the poppies that need fertilizer, the fruit tree getting too much water, the lavender looking dry. He sees the seedling struggling with hard soil, the vine needing more sun, and the blueberries eaten by birds. And he knows he can help. This describes the first model for mentors, the encouragers who walk into our life with wisdom and love, who with a little attention nurture our growth and affirm our journey. This was Donald Bubna – uninvited he walked into my life bringing friendship and encouragement. I have another friend who also is a wonderful gardener. Each year she looks around her community and identifies someone for whom she might be sunshine and water. She comes alongside with encouragement and affirmation and patiently waits to see if a relationship develops. Gardeners do not offer to be mentors, but they are intentional in coming alongside with energy and hope. In this model there is no formal or organizational relationship in place. This is personal. The leader identifies a person who will blossom with encouragement and intentionally seeks him or her out. The response of the potential mentoree will determine if a mentoring relationship develops. In families this is a role often played by uncles, aunts, and grandparents. During my tenure at Regent College this was the model I exercised with the Student Council President. Each year, when a new leader was elected to serve the students, I would take him or her to lunch, offer encouragement and any assistance they would value. Some took me up on the offer for the time of their appointment; some did not. Neale and I began a relationship that continues to this day.

Throughout this chapter I will use names sparingly. There is a reason for this. Mentoring exists only when the mentoree believes that he or she is in a mentoring relationship. Mentors do not make that determination. We may invest ourselves in another, but only the mentoree has the right to call this a mentoring relationship. Thus, I am cautious about identifying persons with whom I have worked unless we have used the language of mentoring to describe our relationship. In most cases we do not use the label. Neale, however, has spoken publicly about our relationship. In Neale's case, our relationship has continued for over fifteen years, ten of which he has been back home in Australia. We correspond now by email and talk by telephone and share a meal when I am down under or he is in North America. But I use Neale to make my point. When the De Pree

Center hosted its first mentoring conference, we invited as speakers Peter Drucker (Max's mentor), Max De Pree, five of us who have been mentored by Max, and we wanted a leader who had been mentored by one of us. I knew that Neale, the highly successful president of a medical center and active in mentoring others, would be an outstanding speaker. We had worked together in what I might call a mentoring relationship for over fifteen years, but we did not use the language. It was with some hesitation that I called Neale and explained what we were looking for and asked whether he saw himself in the role of mentoree. He laughed, gladly accepted, and made a fine presentation at the conference. I tell this story here because the point is important. The mentor does not decide if this is a mentoring relationship. The mentor offers encouragement, affirmation, and wisdom when wanted. It is the mentoree who decides that he or she is in a mentoring relationship. It is the mentoree who calls us mentor.

Advisor In organizational settings, mentors often appear as advisors or sponsors. In the academy, students are assigned an advisor to guide them through the intricacies of the curriculum as they explore potential paths for life and career. Roland Given and George Ladd were my academic mentors, shaping the way I looked at life and scholarship. Organizations often provide sponsors to assist an employee with issues of policy, culture and politics. In this model the mentor is selected by the organization and ideally trained for the role of advisor or sponsor. The mentor is assigned to the employee for a specific period of time or a specific focus of learning. Usually, the mentor guides the student or employee non-directively through the identified stage, serving as a resource and friend. A local high school in Pasadena offers such a mentoring program to its students. Teens are paired with professionals from the community, who are trained "to talk to them, to show them life, how it goes."[5] When both mentoree and mentor are committed, this is a powerful mentoring relationship. However, like all relationships, it takes both persons. Recently, I interviewed a young man and the mentor that his organization had assigned to him. Both were very bright, energetic men filled with hope and promise for the future. The mentor brought experience, wisdom, and integrity to the relationship. The new employee, however, did not see the value of the time spent and chose not to follow up after the initial meeting. The mentor, also quite busy, did not take the time to pursue the relationship and it faded away. Organizational mentoring programs provide valuable resources for new persons and potential renewal for experienced persons, but they will only work if both persons are committed to the learning relationship.

Manager　Within the community of an organization the leadership relationship provides a natural context for mentoring. Leadership is a relationship, a relationship of influence, a relationship in which the leader invests in the person who chooses to follow with the dual purpose of accomplishing the mission and goals of the organization and the development of the follower. It is hard for me to imagine a healthy and effective leadership relationship that is not a learning relationship. Mentoring takes this relationship one step further. Mentors allow employees into their life and work. They give employees access to their thinking, to all decisions. They encourage discussion of vision, purpose, and values. Glenn Barker exemplifies this model for me. As manager, he was directive, teaching me what I needed to learn. As mentor, he was open and vulnerable, inviting me into his head and his heart, allowing me to learn with him in his successes and his failures. Over the years I have offered this kind of access to the people for whose success I was responsible. Some would engage in a learning relationship alongside the managerial one, others preferred only to work. Leslie still talks about me as one of the first mentors in her life, believing in her and giving her the encouragement to pursue her vision for life. She started working for me as a twenty-one-year-old, newly-wed secretary. We maintained a mentoring relationship for five years, meeting monthly to talk about life and leadership. Now she has her doctorate, directs a relationship center with her husband, writes prolifically, speaks around the world, and is someone I refer people to for mentoring. Mentors take great pleasure in watching the people they have invested in realize their potential. Brent started working with me as a teaching assistant. With his gifts and abilities he became a key player on my staff. Early on, Brent chose to establish a mentoring relationship alongside of the managerial one. We met monthly for mentoring conversations in addition to the supervisory meetings of management. It has been a pleasure to watch him grow, pursue graduate studies in management and now emerge as the director of an institutional development program. Managers are in a unique position to mentor, as long as both parties remember that it is the managerial relationship and the shared mission of the organization that defines the relationship within the organization.

Resource   This is the model that defines mentoring for me as evidenced by the previous chapter. Mentorees take responsibility for self-directed learning and seek out mentors as resources to assist them on the journey. The mentoree determines what he or she wants to learn next, seeks out the mentor and manages the relationship as long as it is beneficial to both. This is the model of adult learning.[6] It was the approach I took with Max De Pree. The success of mentoring relationships is directly linked to the initiative of the mentoree. This model starts with that initiative. Over the years various men and women have invited me to walk with them on a portion of their journey. Sometimes we called it mentoring; sometimes we called it lunch. It is an honor and a privilege to be invited into someone's life. But it is also an investment, a commitment not to be made lightly. When Rory Prest asked for access to me for a year, it was a commitment I had to take seriously. We met at least twice each month and spent a weekend together with our families at the beach. But Rory took responsibility to manage the relationship, to make sure he got out of our time together what he needed. When the year was over, I called it an enjoyable learning conversation. He called it a life changing experience. Mentorees decide if it is a mentoring relationship and mentorees manage the relationship. In the end, the mentoree is responsible for its success.

Coach   In recent years executive coaching has emerged as a form of professional leadership mentoring. "Coaching is a rapidly growing vocation these days because so many of us are searching for a qualified person to help us develop and improve.... Coaches help people become more than they realize they can be."[7] An executive coach is basically a resource mentor sought out and engaged by contract to guide the mentoree along a specific portion of the journey. Sometimes coaches are assigned by organizations, but usually mentorees choose them. The relationship with a coach mentor tends to be more contractual and specific about desired outcomes. And coaching often provides a professional service for a fee while mentoring, at its best, is an act of love. But again, this is a learning relationship in which mentorees seek out the mentor coach to guide them through their leadership development. Last year a young leader sought me out to help him reflect on his leadership growth. His organization contracted with me to provide a week of intensive conversation about specific issues of leadership competence and strategy that he wanted to address. An agreement was negotiated up front, in which I would provide testing instruments and analysis, a directed reading list, and two hours each morning and each afternoon over the week to discuss what he was learning. Coaching is a structured form of resource mentoring with a growing number of professionally trained coaches offering their services.

The common thread in all of these models is relationship. A mentor and a mentoree committed together to work on the growth of the mentoree. Relationship is the lifeblood of mentoring. Both mentor and mentoree contribute to the relationship, but only the mentoree will determine whether it is a mentoring relationship or a conversation.

Cultures, gender, and age

Recently, I was speaking in Asia. After my talk, a question from the floor asked the inevitable question: Can you mentor someone of the opposite sex or someone from a different culture? I gave my answer with a smile because sitting in the back row of that room was Patricia, a Chinese woman who has looked to me as a mentor for the past five years. Clearly my response was yes. But the question raises important issues.

The issue of sexuality is significant, and opinions are split. Many would counsel against mentoring across genders,[8] but just as many see the importance of learning from another perspective.[9]

Though it may sadden us, we ought not be surprised that sexuality so frequently becomes an issue; mentorships have a special intimacy, and the bounds are not always clear. Because the teacher holds the power in the situation, the primary responsibility for drawing the line falls in his or her hands.[10]

I cannot imagine giving up the opportunity of learning from Jean or of forfeiting the privilege of learning about leadership development through the eyes of Leslie or Patricia. But the concerns are valid. Shared intimacy can trouble our emotions and distort our motivations. Care must be taken, and while both parties are responsible to manage the relationship, the mentor has particular responsibility to define appropriate boundaries.

While most of my mentors have been men, nearly half of the persons who look to me as a mentor are women. I have learned much from them. But I am careful and do not assume I am invulnerable. Every relationship finds its own form, but in general my mentoring relationships with women take place in public space like a restaurant or an office with an open door. My wife Beverly knows about every meeting and usually has met the person. Similarly, if the woman is married, I like to meet the spouse. The time for meeting is set and we focus on the agenda at hand. The risk is valid but the learning potential of mentoring relationships across gender is rich.

Care also needs to be taken with cross-cultural mentoring relationships. Here it is not so much sexual undercurrent as it is cultural differences.[11] Up front, both persons need to be as clear as possible about the different expectations, the communication of language and behavior, and what is culturally appropriate, especially as it relates to space, values, and time. Both mentor and mentoree need to understand that their questions and their answers come out of a particular cultural context and may need to be translated into the other's world. It is easy to misunderstand a word or gesture from another context, but mentoring across cultures opens up wonderful learning opportunities for both mentor and mentoree. Four of my long-term mentoring relationships have crossed cultural lines and I have learned much from these friends. All of them started with face-to-face meetings, but now are long distance. We connect by email and telephone and visit when our travel paths cross. These have been rich times for me, and I trust of value to the mentorees.

Mentors come in all ages. While the traditional image of a mentor is someone older, wiser, and further along the trail, I think that picture is changing. My Sherpa guides in Nepal were all much younger than I. But they were much wiser about mountains, and in their country much further along the trail. Experience is not always age-related. In organizations the normal rule of thumb is a half-generation of difference between mentor and mentoree.[12] But again, when I needed a financial mentor, I looked to a younger man for whose success I was responsible. Character, wisdom, and experience are much more important than age.

Leadership, management and mentoring

At its heart, leadership is a relationship. In the management of organizations, the development of leadership is greatly enhanced by mentoring relationships because relational leadership and mentoring share a common goal. Both are committed to the growth of men and women to realize their potential and become leaders who influence the people around them.

Leadership is a relationship of influence   It is a relationship in which one person seeks to influence the thoughts, behaviors, beliefs, or values of another person. It is always a relationship between two persons – one who seeks to lead and one who chooses to follow.[13]

Mentoring is a relationship of influence   Gary Yukl, in his book, *Leadership in Organizations*, identifies eleven different ways leaders seek to influence people to follow. He finds powerful influence in relationships of personal identification in which the follower is attracted to a model of life and leadership – mentoring relationships. These kinds of relationship have long range and long lasting influence.[14]

Leadership and mentoring are perceived by the followers Leaders may exercise every model of influence type in the book, but until a follower chooses to accept that influence there is no leadership. It is very important that those of us in leadership always remember that our followers have choice, and that our leadership is always dependent upon someone choosing to follow. This is the reason I hesitate to call myself mentor. I can encourage and affirm, advise and give feedback. I can make a personal commitment to and investment in the growth of another. But only the mentoree has the right to call me mentor, and mentoring occurs only when the mentoree chooses to act on what he or she is learning.

Leadership is a transforming relationship   James MacGregor Burns, in his Pulitzer Prize-winning book *Leadership*, argues that there is an exchange that takes place in every leadership relationship.[15] He calls this exchange *transactional leadership*. He sees the leader and the follower exchanging something. Both gain from the influence type utilized. The followers perceive that it is to their advantage to undertake the requested action, and the leader has set up the request in order to achieve that for which he or she is responsible. Burns sees this exchange present in every leadership relationship. But he wants more. He argues that great leadership is *transforming leadership* in which the leader and the follower grow in the process. The relationship lifts both to a higher plane of maturity, morality, or understanding. Burns wants the leadership relationship to accomplish more than simply making an action happen. He wants the vision, values and beliefs of the follower to be transformed and enlarged, and, in that process, he believes the leader's vision, values, and beliefs will also be enriched. Transforming leadership is leadership that makes a difference in the lives of those involved beyond the task being completed. Mentoring is transforming leadership.

Leadership and mentoring are empowering   Peter Block is a management consultant who has taken Burns's vision a step further in what he calls *empowerment*. In *The Empowered Manager* Block calls for leadership that moves people from dependency to empowerment.[16] He wants leaders to model and encourage empowerment, to use their position to serve and nurture another; one person seeing in another the potential to be more than is visible today and committing him or herself to the development of that potential. This is relational leadership. It is also mentoring.

Good managers and leaders are good mentors Relational leadership is about growing people. It is about promise and hope. It is about men and women realizing their potential and developing into leaders. Not every mentor is a manager; "But, all – absolutely *all* – effective supervisors and managers *should be* mentors."[17] Mentoring is leadership influence focused on growth. Mentoring is the promise of relational leadership, the commitment to a person and a future.

Succession planning is a mentoring commitment Leadership transition is an ongoing concern of every organization. Effective leaders are always grooming persons with the potential to succeed them. For this reason alone every leader should be engaged in a mentoring relationship. Mentoring assists people along their journey and passes on organizational wisdom and culture to the next generation. A friend of mine developed his company from an entrepreneurial idea into a successful partnership with an international corporation. As he reflected on his own journey he realized that one day he would move out to pursue a new vision. So he began the process by selecting a person to mentor. That person of course had to be willing to commit himself to a mentoring relationship. From the beginning their relationship was about mentoring, with a specific focus on equipping the new recruit to take over the leadership of the company. For five years my friend walked with his mentoree, passing on his accumulated knowledge and wisdom, building high levels of trust, with shared vision and values as they weathered the ups and downs of corporate life. And the mentoree chose to learn and to grow into new responsibilities. Today, my friend continues to work with his mentoree, but today the mentoree is president of the company. Mentoring is a powerful process for leadership development and succession planning.

Mentoring is a self-replicating investment of the mentor's hope

The power of mentoring lies in the relationship. Relationships are self-replicating. Max De Pree named three men who were influential mentors in his life. Max was one of many that Peter Drucker has mentored over the decades of his career. Peter invested himself in Max. Max invested himself in me and others. I had the privilege of walking with Rory Prest for a portion of his leadership journey. And the relationships continue. This was brought home to me poignantly in the case of Rory. After the nine months of our mentoring time Rory returned to South Africa with a new commitment to leadership as a "custodian of community." He immediately began to establish relationships and processes to enrich the community of his organization. But on December 21, 2001, less than sixteen months after our time together, Rory had a massive brain hemorrhage and died suddenly at forty-one years of age. I was shocked and am still deeply saddened by this loss, and grieve with his wife Heather and their two young children. This is hard to understand. The loss to his family is enormous. And the leadership vacuum his death created for the national university organization was great. It's not supposed to happen this way!

Rory's death was shocking and sobering and humbling. It casts a severe light upon the mentoring relationship. I didn't know he was going to die! What if I had known that I was investing in the last year of Rory's life and leadership? But I am humbled to have had the privilege to walk a very small part of his journey with him as he thought through his vision, his values and his passions – to learn through him the challenges of leadership and community building in a race-torn culture – to see the particular demands that reconciliation requires of leadership in a wounded and fractured community.

And the mentoring continues. Last year Heather sent me a small book on leadership written by several persons whom Rory had mentored – a book on leadership and mentoring published as a tribute to Rory.[18] In a personal note Heather added that Rory's mentorees continue to mentor the young leaders of South Africa. The mentoring continues. It is a self-replicating investment of the mentor's hope and the promise of tomorrow. Mentoring may be the most rewarding way for a leader to leave a legacy. The promise of mentoring is the hope of the future. We contribute to that future when we invest in the life of another.

An exercise in reflection

The promise of relational leadership is growth. Mentors and mentorees rope themselves together to learn from and with each other. Mentoring is about our investment in another. But it is also an investment in our continued learning and development. The leadership journey is filled with unresolved tensions. Leaders live with constant ambiguity. Mentors walk alongside, encouraging and affirming. Before we look at some of these tensions, it might be good to stop again and reflect. Looking back at your timeline, when did you serve as a mentor? Over the years, who has looked to you as mentor? Who draws on your wisdom and experience today? How are you making yourself available to encourage leadership development? How are you keeping yourself renewed and energized? What do you promise? How do you give hope?

8. Ambiguity

Mentoring reflects on the tensions of relational leadership

When she met me at the restaurant, her gentle character seemed strained with concern. "I have a wonderful new opportunity," she said. "They want me to take over the department for the year the director is on leave – perhaps on a permanent basis after that." That was good news. She was very good at her work and extremely effective in building relationships. She would be a pleasure to work for. "But," she continued, "the assignment has some problems. The director on leave doesn't want any changes made while she's gone. The staff don't like the way things are, but are not very interested in making changes for this year when the future is ambiguous. And senior management wants productivity up and morale raised without creating any trouble with the director on leave. Do I really want to walk into this mess?"

It sounded so familiar. Leadership is full of such tensions, leading diverse constituencies into a shared future. Relational leadership takes each person's vision seriously, always with an eye on the mission. Ronald Heifetz and Marty Linsky see leadership as a risky calling.

Each day brings you opportunities to raise important questions, speak to higher values, and surface unresolved conflicts. Every day you have the chance to make a difference in the lives of people around you. [But] To lead is to live dangerously because when leadership counts, when you lead people through difficult change, you challenge what people hold dear – their daily habits, tools, loyalties, and ways of thinking – with nothing more to offer than a possibility.[1]

Warren Bennis agrees, noting that there are critical passages, personal crises, which every leader must go through along their journey. Business schools do not prepare us for these tensions in life. Mentors, however, can help you work your way through the passages of leadership.[2]

The problem of leadership is that it is never neat and clean. Leadership is filled with ambiguity, pulled by tensions. Leaders are necessary because it is not obvious what should be done. Leaders choose a path and per- suade others to follow without guarantee of success. That is the calling of leadership… and the risk. It is why we seek mentors.

What I wish I had known before I became President

A few years ago the Association of Theological Schools hosted a conference for the presidents of graduate schools of theology in North America who were still serving after ten years. Out of the nearly three hundred member schools, only twenty-five of us had lasted ten or more years. The conference wanted to find out why. Coming out of that time, a small task force was convened to design an executive seminar for new presidents to see if we could extend the tenure of academic presidents. At the task force we discussed eleven tensions inherent in the role of presidential leadership – issues I call "What I wish I had known before I became President." These tensions shaped many conversations with my mentors over the years. They also emerge often as I talk with those who think of me as a mentor. Heifetz and Linsky argue that because leadership contains such inherent ambiguity, it is critical for leaders to have confidants, mentors, with whom they can speak from the heart, knowing that they are cared for, that they will hear the feedback that they need, and that they have a safe place in which to reflect about their choices.[3] It is in mentoring relationships that we find the courage to live in these tensions. These tensions contribute to the agenda of mentoring. I think all of us in leadership need to keep them in mind as we attempt to influence the beliefs, values, actions and behaviors of others. Below are some of the tensions I see inherent in the work of leadership.

A sense of calling and self in the face of conflicting agendas

This may be the most critical issue in leadership. Who are you? Why are you here? Why did you accept this responsibility? What is important? When we accept positions of leadership we accept responsibility for a mission and for a community of people – mission and people, task and relationship – sometimes complementary, sometimes in conflict. Each member of the community has a vision of life, work and mission. And each person has some idea of what role the leader should be playing in their vision. Inevitably, these visions place conflicting expectations upon the leadership – competing agendas emerge demanding leadership action. It is vitally important that leaders know who they are, what they believe, the values to which they are committed, the issues for which they are prepared to fight or resign. Each decision made will please someone and disappoint someone else. To thrive in relationships when people are disappointed with them, leaders must know who they are, why they are here, and what is truly important.

I once asked Max De Pree what he wished he had known before he became CEO. His response was clear: "I wish I had known that the quarterly results of 1985 were not worth dying for. Long-term relationships are much more important. Looking back now I wish I had spent more time with my family and friends!" This from one of the most relational leaders in corporate America. We must continue to reflect on who we have been called to be and what are the important contributions of our lives.

Leaders articulate and model the mission and the culture of their organization constantly before a variety of cooperating and competing constituencies. They must decide often between opposing alternatives. Decisions are made in light of the mission and the values, with the real possibility that they might be wrong. Leaders must know who called them to this responsibility and to whom are they accountable for their life. Who, or what, ultimately determines the value of your life and your work? For followers of Jesus, it is God who calls, and it is a call to service. Your self, your identity, is not bound up in the leadership position you occupy. Your position is only the current opportunity in which you serve God and the people of God's creation. You are not the position you hold. You are a servant of God with a temporary assignment.

Mentors ask: Who are you and who do you intend to be?

Making decisions when you really don't know

This of course is the crux of the matter of leadership. It is why we need a strong sense of self. Someone once defined leadership as the making of decisions when the alternatives are equal. I like that definition. Think about it. If you know that one choice is clearly better, it does not require leadership to choose. Leadership is the risk of choosing when you really don't know, when the alternatives all could be right, or wrong. But we have to choose for the good of the people and the accomplishment of the mission. This is leadership. Leaders are there to bear the risk of deciding when such judgment is called for.

There are two important thoughts that need to be included here: leadership decisions and forgiveness. By leadership decisions I mean those that include the risk of being wrong. Decisions are made at all levels within organizational life. Behavioral decisions, operational decisions, administrative policy decisions, and strategic decisions. The risk increases the more strategic the decision, the more long range the commitment. These are the leadership decisions. Yet all of us know how easy it is to fill our agendas with the low-risk decisions of management to avoid facing the high-risk decisions of leadership. Low-risk decisions should be delegated to the people most involved in the decision. Strategic, high-risk decisions are the responsibility of leadership. Leaders are there to bear the organizational burden of choosing when you really don't know.

And that makes forgiveness an indispensable part of a healthy organization. Leaders will make bad decisions. Organizations that want their leaders to have the courage to choose, the courage to lead, will need to provide a context of forgiveness where mistakes are opportunities to learn, not something to be covered up. If we are afraid to fail, we cannot take the risk to lead. It's that simple. Bad decisions will have consequences that must be addressed, but if we are afraid to try again, we cannot provide effective leadership.

When I was interviewed for the presidency at Regent College, I told the board that I had never been a president before and I assumed I would probably make some mistakes. I wanted to know how they would respond. Would I be out if I made a serious mistake? Or would they help me up, dust me off, and encourage me to keep leading? That provoked a good discussion and may have helped me thrive for twelve years. I made many mistakes, but we corrected, adjusted, apologized as necessary and tried to learn from the experience not to make the same mistake again.

Mentors ask: What is important here? What is at stake? Are there more choices?

Vulnerability, transparency, and forgiveness replacing control, authority, and defensiveness

As we move into the knowledge society, the information era or the connective age – whatever label you wish to use – it is becoming increasingly clear that the old models of authority, control, and power located in the leadership are being replaced by openness, honesty, participation, and power in the hands of everyone. Gone are the days when we believe in infallible leaders. We leave very few people on pedestals for long. It is no longer assumed that leaders will always make the correct decisions. They may carry the responsibility for the burden of deciding, but we all have a stake in their decisions and we expect to be involved. Participants – and that is how we should see all employees – look for transparency, honesty, and vulnerability in their leaders. They want to know what is going on. They want to participate in planning, deciding, and implementing. They are not surprised when leaders make mistakes, but they expect leaders to admit it and even apologize if appropriate. Early in my leadership journey I acted on incomplete, inaccurate information and released an employee. Later, I found that I had been wrong. It was not easy, but necessary, to go to her, apologize, and offer the position back. She returned and excelled in her role. Years later, when she became vice president of another organization, we laughed together (with some embarrassment on my part) as we reminisced on our leadership journeys and growth. Without apology, it is hard for forgiveness to follow. And without forgiveness, as I have already noted, leadership dies.

Leadership is a relationship – a relationship of influence in which one person seeks to influence the vision, values, beliefs, actions, or behaviors of another. It is always a relationship in which power and trust are given by both participants. Everyone leads, not just those in positions of leadership. And everyone follows. There is no leadership without followers. Which means that, in these days of relational leadership, leadership really lies in the hands of the followers. You only lead when someone chooses to accept your influence. Leaders and followers are connected in a living relationship and, like all relationships, it needs care and nurture to maintain the flow of trust and power.

Caring for relationships is something I have tried to take seriously. Followers know we make mistakes. They want to know that we also know our limits. Years ago, I would find surprised employees if I apologized for a leadership error. These days, employees are surprised if you do not admit error, if you do not acknowledge your limitations, your uncertainty, your humanity. At Regent College I was very open about my struggles, my doubts, and fears. People knew that I would ask for help, advice, or confrontation as I learned how to lead. I do not believe that vulnerability and transparency weaken leadership. In fact, I believe that openness strengthens the relationship in which leadership lives and trust grows. When leaders are not transparent and vulnerable in the face of mistakes or even uncertainty, followers withdraw their trust and leadership is diminished.

Mentors ask: What do you fear? Where do you need to grow? What does failure teach? What does trust look like?

Articulating vision with participation of competing constituencies

Max De Pree is often quoted as saying, "The first responsibility of a leader is to define reality." For Max this means vision, but it also means more. Leaders are responsible to lead their organizations in the formation and articulation of a *shared* vision – a vision owned and lived by the members of the community – a vision that drives the daily life and operation of the organization. Reality, however, includes more than vision. It includes culture and constraints and changing environments. Vision is formed alongside and in the context of the organization's culture – its deeply held beliefs and assumptions that control the values and behaviors of its people. Vision is shaped by the limitations of resources, the creativity of people, the focus of mission, and the competing agendas of stakeholder constituencies. And vision is challenged by the constantly changing local and global environment in which the organization exists.

This creates one of the tensions for leadership. It is an exciting challenge to articulate a vision of tomorrow that captures your imagination and inspires your actions today. That is a responsibility of leadership. Actually, I agree with Peter Block, who argues that creating such vision is the responsibility of every person in the community. Everyone works out of their own unique vision, which should be articulated and lived with accountability.[4] But it is Block's point that also creates the tension. Leaders are responsible for organizational vision. But all participants, according to Block, also have a vested interest in an organizational vision that integrates their personal vision. The task of leadership is to weave a tapestry of vision with the participation of all stakeholders recognizing the culture, constraints, and context cradling the organization.

It would be easy to articulate a good vision for the De Pree Center if I did not have to take into account eight board members, ten planning committee members, Fuller Seminary, the donors, and the center staff, all of whom have creative and ever-changing ideas of reality and vision. But this is the task of leadership – to create and articulate vision in a dynamic network of evolving relationships – a task that is never complete, always in development.

And it's always in development partly because the environment in which we are defining reality shifts. The world is changing. Many of us in positions of leadership were educated in the paradigm of modernity with its emphasis on reason, principle, word, and truth. Now we find ourselves leading in a world that emphasizes experience, participation, image, and relationships. The way we have always done things may not be the best way to do them tomorrow. The world we serve is changing, and in this transition time our organizations must keep adapting and renewing. Leaders must understand these changes if they are to define reality for those who follow. Effective leaders will need to articulate visions that engage their diverse constituencies in participatory relationships.

Mentors ask: Why? Who cares? How do creativity and constraint serve each other?

Balancing participatory planning and flexibility for change

Engaging people, however, creates another tension for leadership. Once we work through the tangle of relationships, cast a vision that captures the imagination of the community, and develop commitment to a plan for implementation, we must balance all that participatory planning with a flexibility that embraces change. Much easier to say than do!

Participatory organizations do not change easily. It takes time to generate commitment – and time calcifies and petrifies commitment. Unfortunately, we live and work in a world playing on permanent fast-forward. Everything constantly changes. The challenge for leadership is obvious. Relationships are participatory; planning is a community concert; shared purpose drives the mission; clarity of vision empowers decisions. And everything must be able to change flexibly as the environment changes. That requires a very high degree of trust at every level. Which of course brings us back to the importance of relationship. The only place the supply of trust necessary to sustain flexibility for change can be nurtured is in the one-on-one personal relationships of organizational community. Leadership is a relationship of influence and trust. Shared purpose and relational trust create a dynamic that allows leadership the space for some flexibility.

Glenn Barker was one of my mentors. When he was the Provost and Vice President of Fuller Seminary he was known as a visionary leader who could reverse his position on just about anything. You would think you were following his lead, and the next thing you know he would be heading in the opposite direction and you would have to retool everything to catch up with him. Glenn had a high commitment to purpose and mission and was quite willing to change his mind any time it was for the good of the school. He used to say, "It is not hard to change your mind if you made a missional decision and not a personal decision." He was frustrating to many, but he served a long and successful tenure with significant innovation and growth. He was also highly relational and everyone knew that description I just gave of him. He was trusted to make the best decision for the organization at all times. And with that trust we could tolerate the constant change that surrounded his leadership. Trust is absolutely critical for leadership in today's world.

Mentors ask: What might change? How deeply are you invested personally? Why should people trust you?

Communicating sufficiently to alleviate insecurity and suspicion

In an information age, when people want to participate, people want to know, and they want to know everything. It took me time to learn this during my Regent College days. I am a very open and, I think, transparent person, who talks out loud about everything I am doing. There are no secrets. There are no surprises. But I was continually disappointed to find how often board members, faculty, and sometimes staff and students were suspicious that I would do something without their knowing it. As if I could! When it finally dawned on me that this was an issue of insecurity and suspicion, I began an intensive program of communication. I started with a bi-weekly fax update to the board on all issues before the administration and everything we were working on. This evolved into bi-weekly or monthly email or fax updates to all board members, faculty members, staff, and key donors. Everyone knew exactly what we were working on at any given time. Anxiety decreased and trust grew. It did allow opposition to some issues to take shape earlier, but that also was probably a good thing. Everyone felt included. No one was surprised. And we continued smoothly for the next eight years. I still send out at least a monthly update to my board and planning team at the De Pree Center. Good communications reduces suspicion and grows trust.

Mentors ask: How are you communicating? What are you communicating? How transparent is your leadership? Where does insecurity constrain you?

Comfort with ambiguity and conflict produced by continuous change

Providing leadership in the information age, where people want to know and participate, where everything is continually in change, requires leaders to have a strong sense of self and calling. It also requires a high level of comfort with ambiguity and the ability to transcend and manage the conflict caused by competing visions.

If only leadership were black and white – issues clearly defined – right and wrong standing in stark opposition. But then perhaps it would not be leadership. Leadership lives and breaths and finds its meaning in a world of gray, where issues are messy and muddled, where right and wrong are both present in degrees and open to debate. Leadership is the arena in which men and women have to decide when it is not clear, have to choose when they don't like the choices and have to move forward when the path is foggy. It is always ambiguous. Again, if it were not, we would not need leadership. Leadership is about taking the risk to act decisively in the midst of ambiguity – to frame a reality in which others can contribute with less burden of ambiguity.

And ambiguity, alternative visions, and participating people bring the constant reality of conflict. Conflict, I believe, is not something that happens between people. It is what happens within each one of us when we encounter something contrary to our vision. Leaders today must be counselors of conflict – managers of emotions – persons who can build vital relationships with people with diverse visions, ensuring that each person feels listened to, heard, and cared for. Obviously we cannot satisfy everyone's vision, but participants want to know that their views have been heard, that they have been taken seriously. Effective leaders are comfortable in the presence of conflict – can stand above the debate, engaging in caring relationship with all sides. Again that requires a strong sense of calling, with the ability not to take oneself too seriously.

Mentors ask: Where do you experience conflict? How do you manage conflict? When did you last change? What does flexibility mean?

Developing board and finding governance/leadership balance

Boards play an important role in organizational life. They hold the mission in trust and ensure accountability. The board selects and empowers the chief executive officer. The health of the relationship between the president and the board is vital to the health of the organization. I believe that the stronger the board and the healthier the relationship between board and president, the more effective the organization will be in pursuit of its mission.

While it is the responsibility of the board to select and support the president, I would argue that it is the responsibility of the president to see that the board is successful in its role. The president should assist in the selection, education, participation, and evaluation of board members, as well as the assessment of the effectiveness of the board as a governing body. The president should invest time in each member of the board, ensuring understanding of the mission, culture, operation, and environment of the organization. The president and the board together should clarify the respective roles of leadership and governance exercised by both and protect and ensure effective shared leadership.

I have watched many presidents fail to thrive because they did not take their board seriously and trust was eroded. And I have watched organizations suffer because boards either usurped the leadership responsibilities of the president or abdicated their own governance accountability. The tension in this relationship of shared leadership is dynamic. This is an important issue for leadership. The relationship between president and board, between leadership and governance, feeds the heart of an organization. Like every other relationship it needs to be cultivated and nurtured.

Mentors ask: What does shared governance mean? To whom and how are you accountable? How does the board empower your leadership? How do you ensure the board's effectiveness?

Balancing financial management, revenues and fund raising

Another tension for leaders, particularly leaders of non-profit organizations, arises from the financial side. Leadership charts an optimum course forward through the fragile forces of finances. At Regent College I always felt like I was working within an elastic band with three major forces to manage: tuition revenue, fund raising income, and operational expenses. One of the first two must increase or the expenses have to come down. Tuition revenue could be increased by raising tuition or recruiting more students. Both sources though had their limits – recruitment by space and tuition by competition. Expenses could be reviewed and contained, but too much focus on expenses creates a negative momentum. I have always believed that leaders provide optimism, hope, and positive energy to move forward. Innovation, enthusiasm, and renewal are difficult to attain by cutting expenses. So fund raising was important and it became a major part of my responsibilities, always in a balancing tension with managing expenses and generating revenue.

Financial management is a significant area of tension. Finding the right balance between controlling costs, generating revenue and raising funds touches the leader's relationships with employees, consumers, and donors. A change in one force changes the importance of the others. There is not a "correct" solution, but a solution must be fine tuned each year in the context of the shifting forces.

Fund raising, like every aspect of leadership, is about relationships. And in relationships, clear and honest communication is essential for trust to thrive. Without trust there is no leadership.

Mentors ask: What does stewardship mean? Why do people contribute? Why do you stay in business?

Balancing time for leadership, travel, relationships and personal renewal

Time is a serious constraint for leaders. There is never enough of it and we cannot get more. It is a constraint within which we must live and lead creatively. The management of time, therefore, is always a tension of leadership. It is a tension that permeates every aspect of leadership. There are three areas, however, where I think mentors should keep this tension before us: relationships, family, and personal renewal.

Relationships are labor intensive. They are unpredictable. You cannot manage a relationship; you live in it, invest in it, and grow with it. Relationships are dynamic. And that creates a tension with the more rigid deadlines of organizational leadership. Planning processes, financial cycles, decision procedures, and project timelines fence us in with their fixed schedules, their set deadlines. Leadership is always about living with deadlines, working with schedules. And yet we are always working with people, in relationships. And relationships are unpredictable. People are unpredictable, responding differently at any given moment because of the immediate mix of forces working in their personal lives. This is a tension we learn to live with. Leaders must build into their time space for people and relationships. Relationships must be nurtured, not managed. We must be available to people as necessary, even in the pressure of deadlines. So many times I have had to apologize to people for not being sensitive to the relationship because I was so focused on my immediate deadline. This is a serious tension for everyone in leadership.

Family, of course, is one aspect of this tension. Leadership is consuming. There is always more to be done than you can possibly do with all of the time you have. Leaders are continually making tradeoffs – investing more of themselves in one area at the expense of another – hopefully with intentional balance. I am concerned, however, with the number of families that are damaged by leadership. When we convene gatherings of leaders, particularly CEOs, I am no longer surprised to learn that most of them are on at least their second marriage. The demands of leadership – its deadlines and its relationships – and the rewards of leadership – success and affirmation – so consume the vision and energy of the leader that families often go neglected. Spouses are ignored. Children grow up alone. Leaders must learn to balance this tension. Build in time and space for your family. If you travel, be home by Friday night. Be emotionally and mentally at home often enough to nurture these relationships. Personally, I believe that my life is more likely to be assessed in the long run by the relationships I invested in than by the success of the organizations I led. But again, this is a tension worthy of reflection.

And finally, there is the tension of personal renewal – building in time for reflection and learning, for spiritual encouragement, for physical exercise, for rest and recreation. Many leaders I know schedule their lives so tightly that they are constantly serving without renewing and refilling themselves. I am convinced that your ability to serve others is directly related to your own learning and growth. I see this tension most often with people who travel. Whether the travel is demanding or exciting, they fill their itinerary with activity and return to their organization and family exhausted. Sometimes it is, in fact, the excitement and affirmation of travel that seduces the leader into overbooking time. Traveling is often less ambiguous and thus less risky than leadership in the office. I like to encourage mentorees to watch this tension, to make sure they return from a trip renewed and energized for the leadership tasks awaiting them. This is one tension I work hard on. When I travel, I try to fly mornings, when I can read and think. I avoid red-eye flights. I do not schedule activities both in the evening and the morning. If I have something in the evening, I want the morning free. If I have a breakfast event, I want the evening before free. I need time between activities to reflect on what I am learning, to prepare for the next event, and to center myself before God. I want to be sure I get a full night's sleep and have some meals that are not work related, perhaps even alone. I need time to think. In my case, because I am an introvert, I need space, time away from people. So I always stay in hotels rather than homes. Extroverts often thrive on constant interaction and seek out homes in which to stay; not me. I need some solitude in order to thrive. Each person is different and you will need to reflect on your own balance for this tension. But I would encourage you to measure your success by the energy you bring home from a trip, by the renewed vision and spirit you have to share. Ask your spouse, your colleagues, and your mentors how they see this tension being worked out in your life – because they are watching. And that leads to final point of tension for leaders.

Mentors ask: What is important to you? How healthy are your relationships? What are you teaching your children? What are you learning? What gives you energy?

Understanding organizational culture and the impact of leadership words and behaviors – legacy

Everything you do and say as a leader is being observed. Conclusions are being drawn. People are learning. Your legacy is being formed.

Organizations are living entities with history. They operate with beliefs, assumptions, and values that have accrued over the years to form the organizational culture – that hidden, seldom discussed, set of assumptions and understanding about how we live and work together. The culture of an organization is deeply engrained and operates unconsciously, shaping the behaviors of the people who live and work within its boundaries. People learn over time what works, what is rewarded, what can get you into trouble, how this place really works. The cultural constraints are not necessarily the same as the publicly stated values, policies, and procedures of the organization. They should be, and it is a primary task of leadership to bring stated values and organizational culture into alignment. But you learn about the culture of an organization by watching the actions and behaviors of its people, not by reading its value statement and policy manual.

Edgar Schein, the distinguished professor at MIT's Sloan School of Management, says that perhaps the only thing of unique importance that leaders do is create and shape the culture of their organizations.[5] And that is because everything that leaders do reinforces the values that are embedded into the culture. Every word you speak, every action you take, every decision you make teaches something about what is important. And you are being watched. It always surprised me how often I heard comments about seemingly insignificant activities that reminded me that people were watching – the kind of desk I used, where I parked, whether I paid for my coffee. *Everything we do as leaders teaches. Every moment is a teaching moment.* I cannot stress this enough. Everything you do as a leader proclaims your values to the people around you. If we serve for any length of time in the leadership of an organization, the culture of that organization begins to be defined by the values we live and reinforce. This is part of the legacy that we leave as leaders.

Who we are, what we do, what is important to us is critical to the organization because our leadership leaves a legacy in the culture of the community. How we resolve each of the tensions we have talked about here will reveal our character and underline our values. It will also shape the legacy we leave.

Mentors ask: What legacy are you leaving? What does integrity mean? What would your granddaughter learn by following you around at work?

Living in tension

And this of course bring us back to the first tension. Understanding ourselves and our calling before God and the people we serve is the center from which we address each of these tensions. These are tensions to be lived, not problems to be solved. They are the challenges of leadership that we take into our conversations with mentors. Mentors will not give us answers. More likely they raise additional questions to keep the tension alive. At best they gives us perspective as they share their own journey through the tensions. But mentors give us space to think and to reflect on how we will live in the tensions of leadership. Each of us will live in these tensions differently. But we do so out of the core of our calling, with the conviction of our commitments, with the humble recognition that our leadership leaves a legacy in the culture of our organizations and offers a definition of reality to those who look to us for leadership.

When the woman at the restaurant shared the tensions she faced, I listened, shared the parallels in my own journey and left her with three questions: Who are you? Who cares? and What legacy do you want to leave? Pondering those questions she accepted the position, lead well, and left a profound mark in the lives of many of the staff. And they asked her to stay on and continue to lead them in the midst of the tensions.

9. Inquiry

Mentoring reflects on the future of relational leadership

Questions

The most powerful tool mentors bring to the mentoring relationship is the provocative question. Mentoring is about the art of reflective inquiry. Leadership is about asking the right questions. Max De Pree believes it is through questions that leaders define reality and point the direction. It is through questions that leaders shape the future. It is through questions that we lead people to learn and grow. And it is through questions that mentors encourage leaders to reflect on who they are, what they believe, and what legacy they are leaving.[1]

Peter Block has influenced my thinking about leadership and mentoring. In 1987, Peter wrote *The Empowered Manager*, an excellent book for persons who lead from the middle – as everyone does. He argues clearly for leaders of vision who will take responsibility to lead with integrity from their deepest values. He calls us to lead our piece of the organization the way we wish the whole organization was run. Don't wait to be told. Accept responsibility and act.[2] I still require this book to be read in my classes. When I first read the book I was so impressed I called Peter Block and asked to visit him. At his gracious invitation I flew to the US east coast and spent a delightful day in Peter's home. He was a very encouraging and empowering resource, though technically not a mentor by my relational definition.

A few years later Block wrote the book *Stewardship*, in which he called leaders to accept responsibility for results while recognizing that they have no authority or control. I was sure his point was important but I kept asking, "How do I do it?" He ended the book with the comment that if you have to ask "How?" you didn't understand.[3] It was only after several years as president at Regent College that I began to understand what he was talking about.

In 2001 Peter Block wrote another book, titled *The Answer to How? Is Yes*. This is an important little book because it addresses the power of questions. Block argues that "How?" is the wrong question. It assumes that someone else has the answer, that the solution or strategy belongs to others. How long? How much? How do I do it? are distractions – secondary questions. "How?" assumes someone else has the answers. It abdicates responsibility. The important question is not, "How?" but "Why?" "What is important?" If we know why, if we know what is important, we should choose to do it. "How long?" or "How much?" are not nearly as significant as "What is important here?"[4] Block's book is simple but I think he gets to the heart of the matter. Questions shape our attitude, our leadership, and our future. My wife Beverly has standing instructions that if I come home from work down or depressed, she is to sit me down, put Sarah Brightman on the CD player and make me read Peter Block until I have things back in perspective! It is too easy to focus on the secondary issues and lose sight of what is important and why we do what we do. The effectiveness of our leadership is measured by the quality of our questions.[5]

Questions play a profound role in biblical history. Three questions that stimulate my imagination are asked by Moses, Jesus and God.

Moses is probably my all time favorite biblical leader, perhaps because he is so human. No matter what he did, the people grumbled. It is easy to identify with many of Moses' struggles, right down to the time when he takes the grumbling personally and strikes the rock at Meribah only to be reminded by God that God is the leader here. It's about God, not about Moses. And that mistake costs Moses the completion of his mission. He does not get to enter the promised land. But it is the burning bush dialogue that raises the key question for me. God calls to Moses from the bush and tells him to go to Egypt, negotiate with Pharaoh, and take the people of Israel to a new land. And Moses responds with a question – a question that flows right from his heart and his character – Who am I? Who am I that I should go to Pharaoh and the leaders of Israel? It sounds like a pretty legitimate question to me. But God responds that it is the wrong question. The question is not: Who is Moses? The question is: Who is God? "I AM God. I will go before you and you will follow me."[6] How often, as we live out this leadership journey, we find ourselves asking: Who am I to do this? Moses' question stands as a reminder that it is not about us. We are not the leaders; we are followers. God is the leader. This is all about God.

The second question that captures my thinking is asked by Jesus to his disciples: "Who do people say that I am? Who do you say that I am?"[7] He did not tell them he was the Messiah. They needed to come to that understanding themselves. "Who do you say that I am?" opens the door for the disciples to understand the future. Peter answers for them all, "You are the Messiah, the Christ." It is now their answer, not just his. Jesus had a calling, a purpose, an identity. He called them to follow. They were to continue his legacy. But they had to understand. It had to become their calling, their legacy as well. And Peter's conviction starts him on the path that launches the church and leads to his crucifixion. A simple question, but a life changing answer.

This biblical text carries some content for our understanding of mentoring as well. Jesus formed a mentoring relationship with his disciples. We have a glimpse of it here in this conversation with Peter. However, we read this story in the Gospel of Mark. Tradition suggests that Mark was a disciple of Peter, who mentored him in life, leadership, and faith. At some point in their relationship I imagine that Peter put the question to Mark: Who do you say that Jesus is? And Mark's answer led him to write down the gospel account. And, of course, followers of Jesus who pick up Mark's text believe that the mentoring relationship continues as each reader has to answer Jesus' question: Who do you say that I am? Again we see the replicating nature of the mentoring relationship.

The third question is actually one of the first questions in the Bible. After Adam and Eve had disobeyed God and eaten the forbidden fruit, God comes into the Garden with a question: "Where are you?"[8] It is not as though God needed to be told. But Adam and Eve needed to know. They needed to answer and take responsibility for what had changed in their relationship with God. Questions create opportunities for learning. Learning happens when the answers become ours. And this is the question asked by mentors: Where are you? Where are you in your life, your leadership, your faith? It is the question that opens space for us to understand where we are and where we want to be.

The power of questions is illustrated extremely well by the first question recorded in the Bible. After God has left Adam and Eve to enjoy the Garden with instructions to stay away from the forbidden fruit, the serpent arrives with a question: "Did God *really* say...?"[9] And with that subtle question Satan opened the door to choice and the path to the fall of humanity. And these biblical questions frame the context in which we exercise leadership today: Who is the leader here? To what have we been called? And where are you today?

It is fitting that a book on mentoring should end with questions. I believe the value of this book will be directly proportional to the questions you take away. If I have done my job well, you will close this book with more questions than you had at the beginning. Mentors ask questions. Mentorees reflect on the answers. And that brings us back to the three opening questions with which we started this journey together: What is important to you? What are you teaching with your life? What do you need to know to take the next step? So let me propose several sets of questions for you to ponder as we near the end of this journey.

Measurement

What do we measure?   Max De Pree says measurement is critical to the health of an organization.[10] We measure that which we think is important. What do you measure in your organization? At Regent College we measured applications, enrollment, number of graduates, donations, and expenditures. What do you measure?

What do these measurements suggest are our driving forces? How does this align with the stated mission? Are we measuring results or strategies? What do our measurements suggest is most important to our organization?

One of the companies the De Pree Center is studying –
Flow Auto Companies – intensely measures customer
satisfaction. That is probably why they are one of the top
rated dealerships in the United States. Flow's mission is
not just to sell cars. It is to build lifelong relationships
with people around their automotive needs. Flow also
measures the number of cars repaired that do *not* return.
Technicians are rewarded for fixing it right the first time.
In fact, if you have your car serviced at a Flow dealership,
the technician will call you to be sure everything is
working to your satisfaction. If not, the technician will
drive to your home, pick up your car, leave you a loaner
car, fix your car for free, and return it to your home
cleaned and ready for use! It is no surprise when
customers rank them number one.

How do we measure employee fulfillment?   What do performance reviews teach? What do we learn from them?
Do they measure employee growth? Do they measure
employee satisfaction and fulfillment?

Dacor is a manufacturer of high-end kitchen ap-
pliances. Each year Dacor surveys every employee to
measure employee growth and satisfaction, even down
to the employees' freedom to live out their religious
beliefs in this secular corporate context. Dacor also
conducts an annual values audit, inviting all employees
to measure the company's performance against the
stated values, which like ServiceMaster begin with "To
Honor God in all that we do." The company then designs
its training programs to strengthen both areas. Could
there be a connection here with the fact that Dacor has
experienced 30 percent annual growth for thirty years?

An exercise of inquiry: On a piece of paper, write
across the top the names of three employees for whose
success you are responsible. Now under each name write

their age, then how long they have worked for your organization. Then write the name of their spouse, then the names of their children. Now write down why they work for your organization, then what their dreams and hopes are. You can see where I am going. Leadership is a relationship of influence responsible for achieving results and for building relationships. If we want to lead people, if we expect them to follow, we need to know them – what drives them, their hopes and dreams and passions and how these connect with their work.

What really is important here? What will I learn by watching people at work? What is the connection between voice and touch? Dacor tries to measure this annually. At Regent College we knew we were growing in applications, enrollment, graduation, and outside recognition. But was that our mission? Our mission was theological education – equipping men and women to live and work as the people of God in this world. We say that is important. But do we measure it? To help us get a handle on this we commissioned a qualitative study of students at all stages of their programs and graduates of the college. The study confirmed that people did perceive that they were learning at Regent, but it surprisingly measured something more powerful. The overwhelming result the report revealed was *transformation*. Students who came to Regent were reporting an encounter with God that changed their lives. That is exactly the kind of results we wanted to have. I was not sure how to improve on this, but I believe regular assessment of this type will alert us to the progress we are or are not making.

Leadership

A second set of questions focus on leadership – what is it and how do we develop it? What is leadership? I define leadership as a relationship of influence, a relationship in which one person seeks to influence the vision, values, attitudes, or behaviors of another. Leadership is not a position. It is not a person. I believe that leadership is always a relationship of influence that is exercised differently by different people in different positions. And as I said earlier, it only exists when someone chooses to follow.

And for those of us in positions of leadership, leaders with the responsibility to influence outcomes, there is also that other definition of leadership that I like: Leadership is the risk of deciding when the alternatives are equal. It does not require leadership to choose the best option. Leadership is the risk we take when we must choose and we don't know which option is best. Leadership exercised by senior leaders is an act of personal vulnerability as we risk choice, make commitments, and influence people to follow. Which raises another important question: What is the link between leadership and forgiveness?

Who calls a leader?   God? The Board? The Leader? Followers? Your theology will influence your answer. I believe I am *called* to follow Jesus, *invited* to lead people, and *chosen* to be followed; all of this, I pray, supervised by the Spirit of God.

Where do we look for leaders?   Do we grow our own? Do we grow them for someone else? What are the advantages and the disadvantages of appointing leaders from inside or from outside? Sometimes I think organizations spend too much energy recycling existing leaders and not enough mentoring younger leaders. Thus, again, the question to ponder is: Whom are you preparing to take your place?

How do we grow them once we have them? Do we want someone who knows how to do the job? Or someone who can learn how to do the job? Promotion is an opportunity to learn. Every new position is a new situation for learning. Past experience is important, but might the ability to learn how to lead here be even more important? And of course this raises the question: How risky is learning here? What happens when the leader fails? How do we manage expectations?

Who teaches them what they need to know in order to survive? How do we guarantee their success? Who stands with the leader? Whose fault is it when the leader fails? David Hubbard had a successful thirty-year tenure as the president of Fuller Theological Seminary. Many people believe it was due to the quality of his board and the fact that Max De Pree committed himself to David's success for three decades. Max De Pree considers David Hubbard one of his mentors. I know that David considered Max his mentor – a powerful illustration of the reciprocal nature of the mentoring relationship.

How do we measure leadership potential? One day I sat down with a room full of CEOs to talk about leadership development. Out of that conversation emerged this list of questions to enrich the interview process for leadership selection.

- *Who are their mentors?* Their future leadership will be a reflection of the mentors they have chosen to follow. Warren Bennis recognizes the importance of mentors in leadership development and argues that we do not wait for a mentor to walk into our lives. Leaders need to recruit mentors to guide them. In fact, Bennis goes so far as to say that "one mark of a future leader is the ability to identify, woo, and win the mentors who will change his or her life."[11]

- *Which gods do past behaviors suggest they follow?* When you watch their past leadership and the behaviors of their followers, what gods are being followed? If the model outlined in Chapter 1 is valid, we can tell a lot about leadership potential by watching the people they have led.

- *What is their emotional competency?* Daniel Goleman's work on emotional intelligence offers an important tool for assessing leadership potential. Whether we use Goleman's *Emotional Competencies Inventory* or other means of assessment, it is important to understand the level of a leader's self-awareness and self-management, as well as a leader's social awareness and relationship management.[12]

- *What is their theology of management?* Have they reflected on the theology behind their intended leadership? Have they reflected on the theology being taught by their actions? Do they know the difference?

- *How do we measure integrity of character?* If integrity is the alignment of values and action, voice and touch, we should see their convictions reflected in their leadership relationships. Perhaps we need to develop a 360°-assessment tool to give feedback on spiritual life and personal character.

- *How diverse is their following?* Do they influence only people like themselves? Or do they have broader appeal?

- *Who are they mentoring?* How much interest do they show in growing other leaders?

- *How good are their questions?* Leadership creates the dialogue and defines the future through questions. What are their questions? I encourage leadership candidates to reflect on the questions they want to ask before they are interviewed. A good committee will weigh their questions seriously.

- *What did they do on their last vacation?* Have they learned how to balance work, play, family, relationships, renewal, and spiritual development? If they have not learned this discipline before they accept a senior leadership position, the new position will not offer much opportunity.
- And one final question I like to ask, *Tell me about a recent risk you have taken: What happened and what you learned from it?*

Mentoring programs

Throughout this book we have talked about mentoring as a relationship – two people committed to learning, to growth and to each other. How do we embrace this powerful leadership development strategy within our organizational structures? Sometimes I fear that establishing mentoring programs is as difficult as arranging marriages. But the need for leadership and the benefits of mentoring encourage us to test organizational models. Here are some questions worth pondering if we want to structure mentoring into a company's leadership development program.

- *Why do we need a mentoring program*? What leadership needs have been identified? Is the organization serious about growing its leadership from within? What is the goal of the program? How will it benefit the participants?
- *Is senior management committed to this project?* Will they allocate the time and resources? Are they willing to be mentors? Who must be involved? Who are the champions of the program?

- *Who will be included in this program?* How will participants be selected? Are we targeting a specific level of leadership? Are there certain qualifications that will restrict participation? Will involvement be voluntary or expected of mentors or mentorees?
- *Do we have enough qualified persons to serve as mentors?* Who should serve as mentors? What specific characteristics do we want in our mentors? Will mentors come from outside a person's department? Will we expect two levels of separation in organization hierarchy? What happens if we turn down an interested mentor? How long do we expect a person to be an organizational mentor?
- *What do we expect from the mentor?* What will be the relationship between mentors and managers? Will we provide training for mentors? What does accountability mean here? How will mentors be rewarded in the organization? How should confidentiality be treated?
- *Will the duration of the program be flexible?* What will be the expected timeframe? How much diversity will be allowed in the mentoring relationships? How can an unsatisfactory relationship be brought to conclusion without jeopardizing mentor or mentoree in the organization?
- *How will it be evaluated?* What will success look like? How will mentors be rewarded? How will achievement be celebrated?
- *Who is responsible?* How will mentoring fit with other personnel programs? Who will establish the procedures and policies?
- *What is the cost of failure?* What could go wrong? How does a failed mentoring relationship affect ongoing contribution to the community? What are we teaching if we do not make this successful? What are we teaching if we don't try?[13]

- *Do the advocates of the mentoring program have mentors?*

Organizational health

The fourth set of questions then should focus on culture and work environment.

- *Who are the organizational mentors?* Who are the tribal storytellers?[14] How is the history and culture of your organization passed on? Leaders create and reinforce culture but every organization needs to encourage storytellers to keep the vision alive, to celebrate the traditions, and to revive the history that has shaped the culture. Every year at Regent College the faculty and the new students gathered to tell again the story of Regent's founding and the pivotal events of its history.
- *How does the board define its role?* This is a particularly important question for non-profit organizations. What responsibility does the board have for the success of your organization? What responsibility does the board have for the success of the leader? What responsibility does the leader have for the success of the board? How are decisions made? Where is planning located? Governance and accountability are critical components of organizational life. They are also minefields of potential conflict. The parameters of governance deserve serious inquiry and reflection.
- *How does the organization communicate?* Internally? Externally? Communication is less about knowledge and information than it is about trust and integrity. I am always surprised by the suspicion that organizations have about their leaders. As I noted above, years ago I started sending out a single-page fax (now email) every three or four weeks, just to keep everyone up to speed with everything being talked

about in the President's office. That act alone significantly increased community confidence and trust. It invites others into the conversation.

- *Who owns this place?* In your organization, how are clients perceived? How are donors perceived? How are staff perceived? Is there a hierarchy of value? Whose mission is it? Who are the owners? I had a conversation about this with a young executive in Hong Kong last year. He was surprised that I thought he should have ownership for the mission of the company where he was employed. He said he just worked there. He was even more surprised when I told him that I would never hire him. I don't want just workers. I want owners who are committed to this mission with me.

- *Have we finished the job?* When is it time to close down? Is our mission still vital? What would be lost if we went out of business? It is very difficult for organizations to ask these questions unless of course, they run out of money. But leaders need to be asking both about the organization and about themselves. When is it time to leave? When should the leader move on? That was a question I pondered deeply before deciding to leave Regent College for the De Pree Center. As is the case with most of the questions we have reviewed here, I do not believe there is one answer, one signal that it is time to leave. But I do think there are some symptoms, some pointers: when you can no longer get excited by the organization's vision; when you can find nothing for which to thank God; when you cannot describe a scenario for the future that energizes and compels you; when you no longer see leadership as a place where your calling is worked out; when your personal vision is not compatible with the organization's vision; when you have lost your joy; when you stop learning and growing; when you begin to think you are the leader; when you have run out of questions. When these become your questions, it may be time to risk change.

Vulnerability

Now, just as you thought I was finished, I want to add one final set of questions. *Where are you most vulnerable?* This brings us back to the third question I asked at the beginning of Chapter 1. What do you need to learn next? Or where are you most dependent upon God? I have said frequently that accepting the presidency at Regent College was the best thing I have done for my spiritual development. I had never been a president before. I knew I was in over my head, and it drove me to my knees. I could not imagine beginning a day without time with God, thinking and praying through the day's agenda. I think vulnerability is a good thing for leaders. It keeps us learning and growing. It keeps us dependent upon God. It reminds us that this is not about us. It is about God.

Let's return to the three questions with which we began this journey. I have a fourth question for you. Four questions to ponder as we journey through leadership: What is *really* important to you in life? What do you want to be known for? What do you need to learn next? And one final question asked by Peter Block: What is the question the answer to which will set you free?[15]

Conclusion

"Granddad, if we had been roped up you could have saved me!"

Bubna: What goes around comes around.

Perhaps it has nothing to do with mentoring but there is a circular nature to relationships and community that continues to intrigue me. Maybe it is unique for my particular journey and stops there, but I cannot ignore the connections. Roland Given's son, for whom I babysat, married David Hubbard's daughter. Glenn Barker's son pastors my church. And I now have the significant honor and the pleasure of serving as the director of the De Pree Leadership Center, charged by a board to continue the legacy of Max De Pree.

But the full circle story that still quiets my spirit is Don Bubna, my first mentor from the donut shop forty-seven years ago. When I became the President of Regent College in Vancouver, Don Bubna was senior pastor of a large church south of the city. We crossed paths several times as colleagues in church and education.

By now I understood mentoring and knew that Don Bubna had been a key mentor at a critical stage of my life. During this time my younger brother was murdered, and I again stopped to reflect on life and calling. I decided to take Don to lunch and ask him why he invested so much in me as a teenager. I did and we had a memorable lunch. He responded to my question first by saying that he "saw potential in me and wanted to encourage it." That simple. He saw potential and I found someone who believed in me.

And then he added words that help define mentoring for me. He said, "But this lunch is not about you. This lunch is for me – a gift from God to me. This morning my board fired me over a leadership conflict. Fifty years of leading churches and serving people were discounted this morning and I have been questioning the value of my life and leadership. Now the President of Regent College sits across the table and tells me that my time with him as a young pastor shaped his life and direction. This is God talking to me, and I am grateful." What a beautiful circle of service. What a vivid illustration of mentoring for both of us.

Mentoring is an intentional decision to clip into another's rope, to walk a portion of the journey together. It is a teaching and learning relationship between mentor and mentoree. Both parties contribute; both parties benefit. Who walks your journey with you? To whom are you roped as you develop your leadership potential?

My grandson Brendon is three-years old. He likes me to tell him stories about climbing mountains. One weekend when we were babysitting for him, he brought out a length of rope and asked me to rope up with him. I did and we pretended to climb mountains for a while. I showed him how the rope protects the one who falls, and we experimented using a tree trunk for a belay, impressing him that a three-year old could stop a grown man with a little help from the tree. Later that day, after the rope was put away, Brendon was playing in his yard when their very large Mastiff romped by, and in her enthusiasm, knocked Brendon to the ground. He looked up with large eyes and said, "Granddad, if we had been roped up you could have saved me!" This is the promise of mentoring.

Notes

Introduction

1. http://news.bbc.co.uk/onthisday/hi/dates/stories/september/25/newsid_2538000/2538093.stm. See also Chris Bonnington, *Everest the Hard Way* (New York: Hodder & Stoughton, 1976).
2. Jim Collins, "Leadership Lessons of a Rock Climber," *Fast Company* (December 2003), 106.
3. Edmund P. Hillary, a beekeeper from New Zealand, and Sherpa, Tenzing Norgay, became the first persons to reach the summit of the highest peak on earth, Mt. Everest, 29,028 feet above sea level, on May 29, 1953. On May 16, 1975, Japanese climber, Junko Tabei, became the first woman to reach the summit of Mt. Everest.

Chapter 1

1. Max De Pree, *Leadership is an Art* (East Lansing: Michigan State University Press, 1987), 94.
2. Richard Sennett, *The Corrosion of Character* (New York: W. W. Norton, 1998), 10.
3. James M. Kouzes and Barry Z. Posner, *The Leadership Challenge*, 3rd ed., (San Francisco: Jossey-Bass, 2002), 28.
4. Daniel Goleman, Richard Boyatzis and Annie McKee,

Primal Leadership: Realizing the Power of Emotional Intelligence (Boston: Harvard Business School Press, 2002), 47.

5. James M. Kouzes and Barry Z. Posner, *Credibility: How Leaders Gain and Lose It, Why People Demand It* (San Francisco: Jossey-Bass, 1993).
6. Goleman, Boyatzis and McKee, *Primal Leadership*, 8, 248.
7. Kouzes and Posner, *Credibility*, 12.
8. Edgar H. Schein, *Organizational Culture and Leadership*, 2nd ed. (San Francisco: Jossey-Bass, 1992), 5.
9. Schein, *Organizational Culture*, 228–253.
10. Schein, *Organizational Culture*, 12–14.
11. Jim Collins, *Good to Great* (New York: HarperCollins, 2001), 195.
12. Don Cohen and Laurence Prusak, *In Good Company: How Social Capital Makes Organizations Work*, (Boston: Harvard Business School Press, 2001), 10.
13. Cohen and Prusak, *In Good Company*, 9–11.
14. Joseph A. Maciariello, *Work & Human Nature: Leadership and Management Practices at ServiceMaster and The Drucker Tradition* (Pasadena: De Pree Leadership Center, 2002), 42. Also, Goleman, Boyatzis and McKee, *Primal Leadership*, 83.
15. Eugene H. Peterson, *Follow the Leader* (Unpublished manuscript)
16. Maciariello, *Work & Human Nature*, 50.
17. Jean Lipman-Blumen, *Connective Leadership: Managing in a Changing World* (New York: Oxford University Press, 1996), 22–23.

Chapter 2

1. Peter F. Drucker, *Managing the Nonprofit Organization* (New York: Harper Collins, 1990), 121–124, also *The Effective Executive* (New York: HarperCollins, 1967), 147.
2. 2 Chr. 12–13.
3. Mt. 12:28.
4. Gen. 1:27–8, Col. 1:13–14.
5. L. Gregory Jones, *Embodying Forgiveness* (Grand Rapids: Eerdmans, 1995), 61.
6. Eph. 4:1–7.

7. Eph. 4:16.
8. Robert Fulgham, *All I Really Need to Know, I Learned in Kindergarten* (New York: Random House, 1988), 83-85
9. De Pree, *Leadership Jazz* (New York: Doubleday, 1992), 1–3.
10. De Pree, *Leadership is an Art* (East Lansing: Michigan State University Press, 1987), 11.

Chapter 3

1. Tom Peters and Nancy Austin, *A Passion for Excellence* (New York: Warner Books, 1989), 354–359.
2. Marshall Goldsmith, Laurence Lyons and Alyssa Freas, *Coaching for Leadership* (San Francisco: Jossey-Bass, 2000), 1.
3. Warren Bennis and Robert J. Thomas, *Geeks and Geezers* (Boston: Harvard Business School Press, 2002), xxvi.

Chapter 4

1. Ronald A. Heifetz and Marty Linksy, *Leadership on the Line* (Boston: Harvard Business School Press, 2002), 204.
2. Sharon Daloz Parks, *Big Questions, Worthy Dreams* (San Francisco: Jossey-Bass, 2000), 130.

Chapter 5

1. Gordon F. Shea, *Making the Most of Being Mentored* (Menlo Park: Crisp Publications, 1999), 3.
2. Chip R. Bell, "Mentoring as Partnership," *Coaching for Leadership,* ed. Marshall Goldsmith, Laurence Lyons and Alyssa Freas (San Francisco: Jossey-Bass, 2000), 133.
3. Walter C. Wright, Jr, *Relational Leadership* (Carlisle: Paternoster Publishing, 2000), 2. See also Margo Murray, *Beyond the Myths and Magic of Mentoring* (San Francisco: Jossey-Bass, 1991), xiv.
4. Bobb Biehl, *Mentoring: Confidence in Finding a Mentor and Becoming One* (Nashville: Broadman & Holman Publishers, 1996), 21.

5. Laurent A. Daloz, *Mentor: Guiding the Journey of Adult Learners* (San Francisco: Jossey-Bass, 1999), 176.

6. Bell, 'Mentoring as Partnership', 133.

7. Daloz, *Mentor*, p. 18.

8. Sharon Daloz Parks, *Big Questions, Worthy Dreams* (San Francisco: Jossey-Bass, 2000), 93.

9. Paul D. Stanley and J. Robert Clinton, *Connecting: The Mentoring Relationships You Need to Succeed in Life* (Colorado Springs: Navpress, 1992), 132. While I acknowledge the significant influence that teachers, leaders and historical figures can have on our journey, I would reserve 'mentor' for a person who 'sees' the mentoree uniquely and relates to that unique person and his or her potential. Cp. Daloz, *Mentor*, 214.

10. Jeff Spoelstra, founder of Chat4Teens in California is slowly educating me to the possibilities, noting that teenagers are much more honest and intimate online than in person.

11. Lois J. Zachary, *The Mentor's Guide* (San Francisco: Jossey-Bass, 2000), 34-35.

12. John Schwartz, 'That Parent-Child Conversation Is Becoming Instant, and Online,' *The New York Times*, January 3, 2004.

13. Murray, *Beyond the Myths and Magic of Mentoring*, 133.

Chapter 6

1. Daniel J. Levinson, *The Seasons of a Man's Life* (New York: Ballantine Books, 1978), 40–63 and *The Seasons of a Woman's Life* (New York: Ballantine Books, 1996), 25–27.; Laurent A. Daloz, *Mentor: Guiding the Journey of Adult Learners* (San Francisco: Jossey-Bass, 1999), 43–86; Sharon Daloz Parks, *Big Questions, Worthy Dreams*, (San Francisco: Jossey-Bass, 2000), 37.

2. Edgar H. Schein, *Organizational Culture and Leadership*, 2nd ed. (San Francisco: Jossey-Bass, 1992), 297–333.

Chapter 7

1. Lois J. Zachary, *The Mentor's Guide* (San Francisco: Jossey-Bass, 2000), 163.
2. Zachary, *The Mentor's Guide,* 67.
3. Daniel Goleman, Richard Boyatzis and Annie McKee, *Primal Leadership: Realizing the Power of Emotional Intelligence* (Boston: Harvard Business School Press, 2002), 164.
4. Goleman, 253–256.
5. Gretchen Hoffman, "Plotting a course for success," *The Pasadena Star News* (January 4, 2004), A6
6. Laurent A. Daloz, *Mentor: Guiding the Journey of Adult Learners,* (San Francisco: Jossey-Bass, 1999), 3–5.
7. James A. Belasco, "Foreword," *Coaching for Leadership* (San Francisco: Jossey-Bass, 2000), xi.
8. Bobb Biehl, *Mentoring: Confidence in Finding a Mentor and Becoming One* (Nashville: Broadman & Holman Publishers, 1996), 65.
9. Karol D. Emmerich, "Mentoring the Next Generation of Faithful Leaders," *Faith in Leadership,* ed. Robert Banks and Kimberly Powell (San Francisco: Jossey-Bass, 2000), 111.
10. Daloz, *Mentor,* 104.
11. Zachary, *The Mentor's Guide,* 38.
12. Daloz, *Mentor,* 204.
13. John W. Gardner, *On Leadership* (New York: Free Press, 1990), 2.
14. Gary A. Yukl, *Leadership in Organizations* (Englewood Cliffs: Prentice Hall, 1981), 10–17.
15. James MacGregor Burns, *Leadership* (New York: Harper & Row, 1978), 4.
16. Peter Block, *The Empowered Manager* (San Francisco: Jossey-Bass, 1987), 15.
17. Chip R. Bell, "Mentoring as Partnership," *Coaching for Leadership,* ed. Marshall Goldsmith, Laurence Lyons and Alyssa Freas (San Francisco: Jossey-Bass, 2000), 133.
18. Jack Koma, Motseki Sosibo, Lebohang Ramasike, Ishmael Ndlovu and Ayanda Mbhele, *Servant Leadership* (Johannesburg: Student Christian Organization, 2002).

Chapter 8

1. Ronald A. Heifetz and Marty Linsky, *Leadership on the Line* (Boston: Harvard Business School Press, 2002), 2.
2. Warren Bennis, "The Seven Ages of the Leader," *HBR* (January 2004), 46.
3. Heifetz and Linsky, *Leadership on the Line*, 199–200.
4. Peter Block, *The Empowered Manager* (San Francisco: Jossey-Bass, 1987), 109.
5. Edgar H. Schein, *Organizational Culture and Leadership*, 2nd ed. (San Francisco: Jossey-Bass, 1992), 5.

Chapter 9

1. Max De Pree, *Does Leadership Have a Future?* (Pasadena: De Pree Leadership Center, 2000), 1.
2. Peter Block, *The Empowered Manager*, 107, 123.
3. Peter Block, *Stewardship* (San Francisco: Berrett Koehler, 1993), 234–235.
4. Peter Block, *The Answer to How? Is Yes* (San Francisco: Berrett Koehler, 2001), 2.
5. Jim Collins, *Good to Great* (New York: Harper Collins, 2001), 75.
6. Ex. 3:1-4:17.
7. Mk. 8:27-29.
8. Gen. 3:9.
9. Gen. 3:1.
10. Max De Pree, *Leading Without Power* (San Francisco: Jossey-Bass, 1997), 48.
11. Bennis, "The Seven Ages of the Leader," *HBR* (January 2004), 48.
12. Hay Group, *Emotional Competencies Inventory* (Boston: Boyatzis, Goleman & Hay Acquisition Co, 2002).
13. Many of these questions were suggested by Margo Murray, *Beyond the Myths and Magic of Mentoring* (San Francisco: Jossey-Bass, 1991), 104–105 and Lois J. Zachary, *The Mentor's Guide* (San Francisco: Jossey-Bass, 2000), 168–173.
14. Max De Pree, *Leadership is an Art* (East Lansing: Michigan State University Press, 1987), 76.
15. Block, *The Answer to How? Is Yes*, 32.

Index